PREPPER'S SURVIVAL RETREATS

Your Strategic Relocation Plan for an Uncertain Future

Charley Hogwood

Ulysses Press

Published in the U.S. by:
Ulysses Press
P.O. Box 3440
Berkeley, CA 94703
www.ulyssespress.com

ISBN: 978-1-61243-726-2
Library of Congress Control Number 2017938177

Printed in Canada by Marquis Book Printing
10 9 8 7 6 5 4 3 2 1

Acquisitions editor: Casie Vogel
Managing editor: Claire Chun
Project editor: Caety Klingman
Editor: Renee Rutledge
Proofreader: Shayna Keyles
Front cover design: what!design @ whatweb.com
Cover artwork: from shutterstock.com; mountain house © lcrms; windmill © Robert Heber; barbed wire © Amanda Davis; construction plans © mihalec
Interior photos: see page 167

Distributed by Publishers Group West

I dedicate this book to my amazingly organized and incredible wife Courtney, my loving daughter Natalie, and my baby Tessa, who stood patiently by my side. Without their help and support during the writing of this book, all while in the middle of our own major relocation, this may have well been more of a horror story than a how-to. Thank you each for the wonderful roles that you play in my life.

CONTENTS

INTRODUCTION

We all know what relocating means, but what about strategic relocation? This means planning for the long term; in other words, looking to the future to figure out which location will offer the best combination of safety and survivability while allowing you to continue your normal life. The subject of relocation can be bittersweet. For some, it conjures up images of a fresh start, of greener grass in distant pastures. This is similar to the idea of a short vacation where you say to yourself, "Wow, this place is beautiful/peaceful/fun/amazing. I could live here." For others, relocating is a scary commitment to an unfamiliar place.

In this process, you will face many questions, including "Can I afford it? How will all the pieces come together? What if I can't make it work?" As with any major familial upheaval, you would be wrong to jump into this process based on emotion and/or fear. Strategic relocation happens in steps. You may think it has ended when you sign the papers and someone hands you the key to the front door, but in reality, the process is ongoing.

Efficient relocation is done well before you start driving around with a real estate agent. You must follow through on all things you calculated as important, or you will miss the mark on your intended goals.

This book is all about identifying the best path for you, your family, and your survival group, and how to make wise, informed choices. This is your due diligence. In my years of consulting with survivors and preppers of all stripes, one of the most common questions asked is: "Where is the best place to be if/when things go south?" In other words, when the stinky stuff hits the fan, where do you want to be? The topic can be as complicated as discussing politics or religion in a public square. There are books, blogs, and magazine articles that provide somewhat informed answers. The data is out there, statistics abound, and opinions are many, but in the end, the decision is more than a quantitative analysis: It's about where you really want to be. What is right for some blog author might lead to a life of misery for your family if you don't take the time to measure your desires against your needs and capabilities. Families have been shattered and friendships lost over this topic. But it does not need to be this way at all.

In this book, I will not try to convince you why you should go anywhere in particular. I'm going to present the information I've gathered from years of experience assisting people just like you who have tried and succeeded, and those who have tried and failed. You are you; your family is not typical. That is what makes you great. There will be no-one-size-fits-all answer provided.

Relocating is a major decision that requires careful consideration and reflection. By the time you finish this book, you will have identified what is important to look for in a new place to plant your flag. You will face difficult questions, and you may be disappointed and even frustrated. But I'm not here to sugarcoat anything. If you want that, go to a bakery.

Keep in mind that you are considering preparing for the unthinkable, situations that could be so dire that you want to be as far away as possible and give yourself and your loved ones the best chances of survival.

Strategic relocation is usually thought of as something "those crazy preppers" do because they are worried about the end of the world. In reality, any family that considers a move can benefit from careful thought and research of the new area. Would you knowingly move to a home downwind of a nearby landfill? Would you build a house on the cheap property alongside that old chemical plant? Do you think moving to those one-dollar houses in the dilapidated areas of Detroit, where the police won't even patrol, would be a wise decision? As much of a great deal it may be to buy up acres on a Superfund cleanup site, who would be comfortable letting their children swim in those ponds on a sunny afternoon?

As I said previously, I am not going to identify survival utopia and send you there; I am going to help you flesh out the most appropriate location for your family or group, because until the balloon actually goes up, you need to live a normal life. What does this mean for you? This means looking at several different topics, including finances, relocation goals, and your long-term survival needs, all of which I'll cover in this book.

Simply put, whatever your reason for picking up stakes and pitching your tent elsewhere, you want to carefully consider what you are getting into, and if you can maintain a comfortable lifestyle until all hell breaks loose.

CHAPTER 1

A BRIEF HISTORY OF COLLAPSE

The United States has long been the undisputed champion when it comes to economic power. The thing about power is that no one keeps it all forever.

There is a lot of global economic uncertainty, and with the globalization of goods and services, nations have become inextricably intertwined. Some nations are bigger than others and quite a few spend a lot of time teetering back and forth from a variety of problems, from bad luck to all-out corruption. This means that we have to be careful to avoid a domino effect, where changes in one nation's politics or government could mean disaster for us here. Here's how the US compares to other countries that have experienced serious unrest.

RUSSIA

When the Soviet Union fell, it came as a bit of a surprise, even though the West had been trying for decades to make it happen. Russians live in a system that gives to the Fatherland first, and they are taught to accept whatever is left for their family. They are used to famine and having few resources, and for the most part, they will tolerate it because they are a proud people who expect that, eventually, things will get better.

The difference with Americans is that we are, typically, more individualistic. We want to be represented in government but our independence must come first. We are a "me first, then the government gets a little bit" society. While Russia has experienced collapse, we really have not. So what does this mean, in such volatile economic times? It means that if a serious contraction in the economy or a severe national disaster were to occur, our population might come unglued faster than the populations of countries that do not share our level of wealth and convenience, for the sheer reason that suddenly not having the familiar first-world luxuries would lead people into chaos.

SOUTH AMERICA

Argentina, Bolivia, and Venezuela were at one time the economic stars of South America. However, they all have something in common: They have all suffered from total economic collapse. There were multiple reasons for collapse, including government corruption, poor economic policies, and lack of domestic product production.

The crisis in Argentina happened between 2001 and 2002, around the same time we got seriously preoccupied with our response to the 9/11 terrorist attacks. Because of this, most Americans had no idea of what was happening in South America. It was only later, as we began to ask questions of our own due to the so-called Great Recession, that we took notice of the follow-up effects of a collapse in a relatively modern nation.

As those South American countries began to fall, many people saw increased unrest and crime in the cities, so they moved to the country and the hills. (Sound familiar? The top-ranking retreat dream in our country is a remote place out in the hills.) What's the problem with this mentality? In Argentina, people found that running to the hills led them right to the very problems they were trying to avoid. While the economy was collapsing, security forces faced pay cuts and loss of personnel. In an effort to reconstitute their forces, law enforcement was forced to withdraw from the outskirts and bring order to the city centers, the lifeblood and population centers of the country. Those people who left the chaos and uncertainty of the city were now left to fend for themselves. Crime goes where it can operate with the least interference, and it festered in the places where the government ceded control. Gangs and organized crime had almost free reign to operate as they saw fit. The irony of the situation was that as the government forces focused on the cities, many urban areas became safer than the suburbs or rural areas because of the increased law-enforcement presence.

Later in the book, we will dig into what kinds of crimes and behaviors happen in those remote areas when no one is coming to help. You will be able to make better informed decisions as to where you should aim to be when you can no longer depend on help coming (or when the "help" is not who you were hoping for), because there is always someone to fill the vacuum of authority, whether you like it or not.

WHY IS THIS RELEVANT?

As we say in survival, people will always be your biggest problem. To understand what you need in a survival property or strategic relocation, you need to understand what the people who have been through a serious community survival event have experienced. You can imagine and speculate about how a societal collapse might affect you, but history offers a more accurate perspective. Though there are many less-than-accurate doom predictors out there, bear in mind that a lot of times, their only experience in disaster is based on their own imagination.

Research shows that there are commonalities among community collapse events, and if you know where to look, you will see indications earlier than most other people, giving you an advantage with respect to timing and preparation.

I will not delve too deeply into the topic of systemic failures, but introduce the concept as evidence that they can and do happen more often than you might realize. The United States is certainly more prepared than most countries due to our robust emergency management and information systems, but these programs also breed complacency and a dependence on the government to always be there for us if the lights go out. We need to fight this normalcy bias because, as well-prepared as our nation is, emergency response teams cannot be there for everyone due to sheer population numbers. On a good day, we might have one first responder per nearly 1,000 citizens, and during an emergency, many of those responders are grouped into a single emergency/disaster area. It really is up to you to prepare yourself as much as possible and try to be located in an area that would have the least negative effect on your family and business.

None of us has a crystal ball, but if we can look up from our devices every once in a while, we should have an idea of what to look for. There will always be societal noise, but if we begin to hear some key indicators of disruption or increased news discussions regarding some of the following topics, that could be an indicator of bigger things to come. These are commonly recognized as triggers and may be a preview of difficult times ahead.

- Hyperinflation
- Bank holidays
- Slowing economic growth trending over several business quarters
- US Reserve currency being sidelined by other nations. The US dollar is a globally accepted currency, which keeps its value up and gives it credibility in other countries. However, if, for example, global commodities such as oil were to switch to Chinese currency, it would shake the confidence of the American financial system.

- Serious discussion by banking systems about seizing savings accounts. Why would the bank even talk about this? This is an emergency plan to put money back into the economy or pay down debt, if necessary.
- Haircutting personal accounts by banks. This has happened in recent years in places such as Cyprus, where the bank went into private accounts and arbitrarily withdrew money without consent.
- Home sales and construction continuously falling
- Home foreclosures increasing

There is not much you can do about the overall macroeconomic situation, but you do have some control over your family's situation, so you need to focus on what you can control and prepare.

For more reading on how communities and nations fall into chaos, do some research into:

- Current events in Venezuela
- 2011 earthquake, tsunami, and nuclear plant meltdown at Fukushima
- 2004 Indian Ocean tsunami that devastated multiple countries
- Historical earthquakes in the western US
- Chernobyl meltdown that created a massive human exclusion zone
- Sarajevo, once a wealthy Olympic city, that in 10 years became a no-man's-land in a major civil war

The list goes on, full of places that have fallen with great human toll.

If you are looking for reasons to validate your decision to relocate to a safer place or a create a Plan B, those reasons are everywhere. These are just the big ones: events that are considered low frequency, yet high impact. There are countless other, more marketable reasons to convince friends and the average, unconcerned family members to get on board. The usual motivator is food. As long as people have comfortable access to food, they will put up with a lot of inconvenience and corruption. Let the food dry up, and it's time to put on a helmet.

Let's jump in to how to get off to a great start with your strategy.

CHAPTER 2

WHAT DO YOU NEED TO SURVIVE?

To end up where you want to be, you need to build a map to help you get there. For most of us, relocating is more than just riding into the sunset until we find happiness. While some people are nomadic and have few responsibilities, the rest of us are bound to reality with work, family, and financial limitations. If you are indeed one of those nomads, this book will still provide more than enough information to help with your life on the go. Most people will use this book to make wise choices, save great amounts of time and money, and wrap their journey up with a feeling of a job well done, all while sipping a refreshment at their new abode.

EIGHT MAIN AREAS OF SURVIVAL

Regardless of where you end up, you will need all the same things for survival, and the more your property can provide or support, the easier your life will be. There are eight main areas of survival that you must work to satisfy.

1. Food

2. Water

3. Shelter

4. Health and safety

5. Security

6. Energy

7. Communication

8. Transportation/accessibility

Normally, the eighth area of survival is transportation. You have to know how you are going to get your group and all your gear from point A to point B. However, in this book, as it relates to properties, we're going to be looking at the *accessibility* of a piece of property so that you/your family/your group/your gear has someplace safe to ride out the storm.

FOOD

Food is a key requirement in survival. This goes without saying. But now that you are looking for a place to survive long term, you will need to decide if you can produce and harvest food at this location.

There are two things the survivor will need in the longer term: carbohydrates and protein. As you consider a property, it would be wise to explore the bioavailability of the area and the specific location. Factor in the local climate, soil conditions, and seasonal availability of sunlight.

You will also need to determine how large your garden needs to be to provide enough food for your family. Is there enough space?

Will the soil need to be amended? Is the ground rocky? Has there been any ground contamination?

When analyzing protein sources, consider what types of meat could be harvested from the local area. And consider whether other people in the area are looking at the same protein sources as you are. Are there other hunters, which would reduce the availability of animal meats? For example, during the Civil War, the deer population was decimated by hungry armies that needed to be fed, but locals had counted on that meat as part of their diet.

Can you raise livestock here? If so, you'll need to calculate grazing space to figure out if the land can support large or small livestock, or if you will need to bring in additional feed to offset grazing potential. It's also important to find out about any

Aeroponics

regulations restricting animal ownership. If all else fails, you can raise more than enough rabbits and no one would ever know, even in an apartment or bunker.

If you are knowledgeable about wild edibles, it would be helpful to survey for any existing or possible wild edibles, or maybe even consider adding some permaculture to the land in the future. This may also include medicinal plants.

If nothing is available, there are always aquaponics, aeroponics, and sprouts as alternative food-production strategies. I do not promote hydroponics as a solid option due to the equipment and energy requirements these systems need to operate.

Be careful to not overestimate the opportunities to live off of the land, as flora and fauna are finite in their existence and reproduction cycles. They are also susceptible to the same hazards and perils as humans.

Climate matters. In the South, such as Florida, there is always a growing season for something. In more northern regions, the growing season is much shorter. If you want more information on growing zones, a simple internet search will explain the growing seasons and which crops do well in different climates.

WATER

Water is the source of all life, and to the survivor, it is a critical resource. A deal breaker on a location would be the absence of usable water on, or safely near, the property. End of story. Water is a heavy 8.3 pounds per gallon. In a survival or off-grid situation, a large amount of time and effort could be spent procuring and preparing water for the various tasks of daily life. Since water can be cumbersome to store, it would be a good idea to locate a property that has at least one, if not two, natural sources to utilize.

However, it is not the end of the world if water is not directly on site, but you will need to take this into account if your plan is to travel to a nearby source and transport it back to the homestead. Once you locate a water source, ask:

- How close is the water source to the home site?
- How close is water to the garden area?
- How close is water to the animal pens/barn?
- Is the water in the form of a stream, creek, or river?
  - If so, what is the potential of accidental or intentional contamination? Is there a problem neighbor upstream who might toss a dead animal or chemical in the water to render it unusable? (This is just to demonstrate why a protected source is a good idea.)
  - Would you face any hazards or threats while traveling to collect water for transport back to the homestead?
  - Is flooding of the garden or home site possible?
  - Will the water source freeze or dry up in the different seasons?

There are ways to supplement your water needs by catching rainwater using a large container storage. In many areas of the country, just one heavy rain has the potential to satisfy your annual water storage needs if you utilize enough surface area and funnel the water into storage. You will need to properly prepare the water for any sanitary needs once it touches an unsanitary surface, but there are many survival tasks that do not require potable (drinkable) quality water.

A well would be a very secure form of water production as long as the groundwater is not contaminated. It is not unreasonable to check the aquifer depth and direction of flow to see what exists upstream that might affect your underground water.

Installing a well is a great potential option, but there are some important considerations.

- **Depth of usable water.** Is it at a depth that you can reasonably and affordably reach?
- **Water/mineral rights.** You better check whether or not the property purchase includes them before you count on it.
- **Depth of water table/aquifer.** Can it be pumped with an off-grid pump option, such as a solar or hand pump? This will take some preplanning and positioning of materials so you can be ready to switch your well over to the alternate plumbing in case of grid or power failure.

Digging a well

A possible option, depending on the water table, would be to dig a pond, as long as it will fill and stay filled. If there are areas where it appears that water has stood or the ground is muddy or you see the types of vegetation that grow in wet terrain, you should be able to dig a pond or perhaps an open well. This all depends on the recharge capability of the soils and water table.

Storage solutions will include rain barrels, cisterns, and farm tanks, as well as the newer waterbed-style bladder tanks located under the home. Even swimming pools of various size and construction are useful to store water.

Keep in mind that it is okay to bury some of these storage systems for security and concealment, and to make ground surface space available for other needs. Just be aware of surface loads above any underground facility or storage. Burying can also maintain a safe temperature, which can reduce freezing and bacteria loads if sealed properly. Burying can additionally protect the storage container from the sunlight and physical damage. When back filling the holes around these tanks, prevent rocks and sharp objects from impacting the containers.

SHELTER

Protection against the elements is one of the basic human needs. It is also something that we take for granted and even underestimate in our modern lives. Regardless of location, you will need to find a way to manage your climate in order to regulate your core temperature within a safe operating range, just like you would with any other piece of equipment.

Under normal survival circumstances, you might be looking for shelter on the fly, or even constructing protection from the elements with materials you scavenge. But since you are taking the proactive step to strategically relocate, you have the time and opportunity to find a property with a shelter or home in place. If you prefer to find a place that does not have such a shelter so that you can park a camper or pitch tents, it would be wise to survey for potential resources that could be used in an emergency. If you are even more ambitious, you may want to build your own place, such as a cabin.

When surveying a property for shelter resources, keep an open mind. Try to not overestimate your skills and underestimate your long-term needs.

HEALTH AND SAFETY

This is part research and part crystal ball. The very reason you are strategically relocating is to put yourself and your family in a place of relative safety. The property you are considering should provide, or support, health and safety. At the very least, it should not contain any substantial health threats or be located anywhere that nearby hazards could jeopardize your family's health. These include nearby or upwind hazards, such as chemical plants, dams, flood potential, radiological sources, or even nuclear/radiological targets in wartime. Distances and wind patterns should be accounted for if these are a concern. Population density and potential for disease may be a health consideration.

Demographic makeup of surrounding areas can also be a potential hazard if you are not aligned with the majority population. This includes socioeconomic status, race, religion, political views, and other dividing factors. This does not only apply to the well-off. There are plenty of historical examples of lower-income populations being driven from their homes or not supported in disaster scenarios by wealthier communities.

Essentially, you might wargame various scenarios that align with your particular preparedness agenda prior to beginning your property search to determine what health- and safety-oriented threats are important to you.

SECURITY

In survival, security is a consideration that should be placed at the top of your priorities. Without security, you are only holding onto your things until someone comes along who wants them more than you do.

When surveying a property for security potential, you need to think in terms of limiting the opportunity for trespass, any ease of advance against your structures and equipment, cover and/or concealment of invaders by way of blind spots, and the opportunity to use existing or added channeling features.

- Does the property have any security advantages, such as higher ground or natural terrain features, that would delay or complicate personnel or vehicles from approaching?
- Is the property situated in a fashion that would allow friendly neighbors to keep an eye on things while you are

away, or is it concealed from view entirely? Can you use this to your advantage in your security plan?

- Will your regular activities draw attention from surrounding properties (i.e., shooting, gardening, group gatherings, etc.)?
- How defendable is the property? Is it too large for you to manage? If so, can you create a smaller perimeter within the overall property?
- What is the likelihood of transient traffic wandering through your property? Is this property positioned between two other populated areas, leading people to use it as a potential shortcut?
- Is this property close to a highly traveled route, such as a highway or hiking trails?
- Is this piece of property such that it may be on someone else's radar as a good place to retreat to? If so, would you be forced to regularly confront other people on your land?
- Is this land known as a good hunting location that others may want to use?
- Are there any other camps, settlements, or competing groups in the area, to your knowledge?
- Is there any indication or reasonable possibility of an increased threat level in this area?
- Are there any natural hazards near or upwind of this property that could adversely affect you (i.e., flood-prone waters, wildfire potential, falling rocks, landslides, extreme weather, a dam nearby, etc.)?

ENERGY

When most people think of energy, they automatically think electricity. While electricity is our most common form of energy in the modern world, there are alternatives the survival-minded family should consider in the event of total grid failure, or damage. Damage could range from large-scale events down to something as simple as a tree falling on a nearby powerline.

Electricity is probably one of the easier energy resources a prepared family can live without or work around. Humans have survived just fine for millennia without it and reliable power has only been available in the modern world for a short period of time. There are many countries around the globe that carry on daily with little to no electrical support.

When evaluating a property for long-term survival, look for a useful alternative energy solution, such as solar, wind, moving water, biofuel, and especially firewood.

COMMUNICATION

In survival, communication is not restricted to verbal language. Communication is part of a total package that includes everything from transport of information physically, by person or message, to radio signals. It may be tempting to hole away in the woods and avoid everyone, but by doing so, you are severely limiting your survival capabilities.

There is no way for any one person, family, or survival group to thrive without some form of outside assistance. This not only includes lacking materials, but skills that you and your family will not have. Most importantly, you should start looking into different forms of intelligence gathering, and how they can help you learn about a potential relocation environment. If you don't have one yet, it's important to develop a network of friendly agents who are all communicating during the evolving situations you will face so you can remain ahead of any trouble in the form of people, community leadership, and even illnesses that may be moving around in your area.

This is all facilitated by strong communication capabilities. The property you are looking at should support this by being located within reasonable commuting distance to those who would be considered friendly contacts or allies.

Such trips should be possible year round and not restricted by seasons, unless you have serious off-grid capabilities and must wait out an entire season; for instance, locations that have high winter snow accumulation.

A property would ideally be on a higher ground that would support radio communications. While this is not always possible, you may be able to offset this condition with the addition of antennas or repeaters for wireless communications. If you are looking at an urban location, your radio signals may be blocked by building construction. However, you can work around this by rooftop positioning or by creating a radio relay network, if needed.

Communications will be beneficial if you are in support or need support of neighbors during regular or emergency operations. Can you reach the neighbors by foot, vehicle, or radio from your location in an acceptable timeframe?

TRANSPORTATION/ACCESSIBILITY

Having good access to the property dovetails with communication. Keep in mind that the same avenues of approach that get you there will get trespassers there as well. You do need access, but you will need to account for all access points and routes in your security planning. This means any trail, drive, right of way, waterway, or other clearing that will allow foot or vehicle traffic to pass or approach should be observed and possibly delayed as part of your 4-D security plan (see page 89). Here are some questions to consider:

- Is there year-round access to the property? How much maintenance will the access road or trails require? Is there flooding or debris blockage potential?
- Does your approach pass by a threat or hostile area?
- Does the property have more than one access that can double as an escape route in an emergency? If not, can one be created?
- Can emergency vehicles/firetrucks service the property? The types of soils, bends in the road or driveway, and low-hanging trees may prevent rescue and construction vehicles from getting close enough to do their work.
- How far off the regular roads is the property? If you need to go to work or school, will the access roads take too long to transit? Is the property just too far from everything?

You will never find a property that offers all the perfect solutions and conveniences you would like. But as long as you know what you are getting into, you can make educated decisions about how much improvement will be needed to make a location the best place to be, or decide to let it go and continue the search.

* * *

There are some things in common between relocating to a place for daily living and relocating for survival. For everyday life, you will need resources, just as in survival. Since we are attempting to strategically relocate for survival, we will look at those needs first.

The key to survival is to identify your priorities based on your situation and work to provide a solution to all these areas of survival in an evenly scaled fashion. Stated simply, focus on each area in a balanced manner. There is little sense in storing several years' worth of food if you have no way to prepare or protect it. When people hear protect, many will default to the idea of needing thousands of rounds of ammo to defend their stocks. While ammo is important, so is the place you are going to store your food. Your survival retreat is the shelter, where all of your hard-earned supplies will find protection. It is important to get it right based on what your survival scenario calls for. This is where strategic thinking comes in.

CHAPTER 3
THE BIG QUESTIONS

Since you are thinking strategically, you need to have a clear vision and understanding of why you have decided to relocate or set up a retreat. You need to define the big picture. As soon as you present this idea to anyone, there will be questions. If you cannot answer those questions in some coherent manner, you will lose the opportunity to get everyone on board.

WHY

Before diving into searching for a piece of property, you must first gain a clear understanding of your wants and needs. Importantly, you cannot convince others to join you until you know why you are doing this.

What is it you *think* you are looking for in a relocation property? Have you watched too much TV and thought to yourself that you want a fully stocked bunker as soon as possible? Does the idea of a secret lair hidden under an innocuous cabin in the woods get you excited? Maybe you just want to check out of the rat race and move to a mini-farm 100 miles from everywhere. Let's face it, who hasn't seen the commercial about starting an alpaca farm and thought to themselves, "I can do that; how hard could it be to raise cute furry animals and sell the wool for enough money to live happily ever after?"

This may be reality check number two, right after telling your wife you want to buy a bunker for the coming invasion. I don't have anything against alpacas, but it would be a good idea to think long and hard before leaving your job as a computer whiz to be a fur farmer.

Just as the foundation of your house is critical for it to withstand the storm, so are the reasons you are moving. Don't cheat yourself by glossing over important needs with emotional decisions. Be truthful, and answer the following questions out loud so you can hear if you make any sense. It might take some refining until you are able to present a coherent answer to the questions you are likely to get asked.

- Why are you doing this?
- What do you expect to gain by relocating?
- Are your reasons to move realistic?
- Are you sure this is not a knee-jerk reaction to something?
- Is this move good for the family? Why?
- Are you in a position to move now? When will you be?
- How will your family receive the idea?

Other questions may come to mind, and that is okay. I just want you to internalize the idea of relocating. When you are comfortable with the idea, you will exude confidence and passion, and this will aid your cause well.

HOW

The next step is to visualize the move so you can more easily spot any gaps or blind spots in the plan. How often have you had some idea that you just had to try and then, once you got into it, you realized it sounded better in your head than it turned out in real life? A relocation has a lot of moving parts. It will go so much smoother if you take the time to address any internal confusion.

You need to consider all your responsibilities. Moving to the woods may sound like a great idea, but life has a way of yanking us back into reality. Some of the first questions you will hear will be in regard to family and work, so make sure that you have answers ready to go.

WHO

If something bad does happen, who do you expect to arrive at your new place in an emergency? If your place is the designated retreat location, you'll need to think about available space to house and care for everyone. How will relocating affect others?

Here is a list of considerations you will need to address.

Children. Uprooting children is fraught with emotional challenges. Younger kids may be able to make a move easily, but once they are in the upper grades of school, they may have ties that are nonnegotiable, as far as they are concerned.

Elderly family members. Older family will eventually require care at a level that you may not be able to provide while living in a survival retreat. What is your plan for this? You may want to consider how far you are willing to travel for medical care in the future. This should be a major consideration, regardless of who is going with you.

People with special needs or with disabilities. This question is similar to the ones regarding children and the elderly. If you need durable medical equipment or backup electrical requirements, put these on the list of important things to work out.

Animals or pets. There are many factors to consider when moving animals to a new place, such as climate, housing, rules, vaccinations, zoning, etc.

Friends and extended family. What about everyone else? Will you have extended family, in-laws, grandchildren, or family friends tagging along? How about survival group members? It may be a wise idea to establish rules on housing and caring for others ahead of time, though a little further on in the process.

WHEN

Timing is everything in a move. How soon do you want to make this happen? If society is crumbling before your eyes, you are probably no longer strategically relocating. In that case, you are now *tactically* relocating. What's the difference? Strategic means to plan ahead of time at a high level, giving yourself the best possible position for an anticipated situation. Tactical planning is more ground level and requires constantly improving your position, gaining an advantage in the short term. If strategic planning is relocating to a specific area for a future scenario, tactical planning is the placement of fortifications, defenses, and survival measures at that location as the situation requires.

WISDOM TIP

Keep in mind that if you tell friends that you are buying a retreat and are preparing for a major disaster event, if the event really happens, you may get some unwanted company knocking on the door. It is harder than you think to run off old friends with a shotgun when they show up hungry or injured. We have all heard the story about the family who came for dinner and didn't leave. Well, if you tell people you will have food when no one else does, you will have plenty of people over for dinner, and they won't leave until the food is all gone.

For most people, planning will take months or years. Like a game of chess, you will need to move all the pieces of your life into the position for success. Some examples: waiting for the kids to finish school, waiting to retire, or waiting until you are financially able to walk away.

Another question that may greatly influence your timing is whether the new location is going to be a primary location or a secondary location. If you are planning to pick up and move completely and permanently, there will be many considerations to address, such as employment, commute times to work, kids' schools, etc.

A secondary location is more of a Plan B type of thing: a location that is in your back pocket that may not demand as much planning or preparing right away. Many people will set up a retreat and use it to vacation until the time is right to move there full time. There are several options that can make this a suitable compromise. If the new location is in an area where rentals are popular, you may be able to collect some income to offset the costs of ownership. Vacationers renting your property will likely not consider your place as a retreat, since the thought of anything bad happening probably never crosses their minds.

Try not to leave any clues as to the real purpose of the retreat for vacationing eyes to see.

WHERE

In the real estate business, they always say "location, location, location." That old adage holds true in planning for your survival as well. Whether you are on the run or strategically planning your retreat location, you must carefully consider where you will be sleeping. Remember, there are eight main areas of survival you should be looking for in a piece of land or survival property. Use the list provided in Chapter 2 when you are considering a piece of property. You may not find a property with the perfect combination that provides for every need, but if you know what it does have, you may be able to adapt for those characteristics the property does not have.

The amount of time you expect to be on site will also determine which characteristics are more important. For example, if you were only going to be there for a short period, the capacity to grow food would not be as important as the security the property may provide. Keep in mind that everything in survival is a trade-off. The sooner you (and your family) embrace this, the easier your decision-making process will become.

For now, here's a quick refresher:

1. Food
2. Water
3. Shelter
4. Health and safety

5. Security
6. Energy
7. Communications
8. Transportation/Accessibility

Realistically, there are several location options available for the future survivor who wants to relocate:

- A farm
- Empty land to either camp on or build on
- A new or existing home on some amount of land
- An underground bunker
- A compound (usually consisting of facilities or buildings to house multiple people)
- A city location to hide in the crowd
- A boat

Other than the boat idea, which I won't go into since it is a specialty scenario that is always relocating, these choices fall under three options: urban, suburban, and rural. What type of situation are you looking for?

Be warned, the type of situation you *think* you're looking for may very well change as you start to gather information. Be open minded and willing to adapt as necessary.

RURAL RELOCATION

The go-to plan I always hear about is the ever-persistent "heading for the hills" scenario. In bad ideas, this is only preceded by a plan to seize a local Walmart and wait out the apocalypse.

There are many challenges with the plan to head for the hills. Most notably, those who already live in the hills probably do not want you there. If you have ever felt the anguish of being picked last for dodgeball, that will pale in comparison to blindly showing up in a small country town where everyone knows everyone and no one knows you, that city person who wants a piece of their little slice of privacy.

It's not to say that you can't make such a move, but it will be imperative that you work to make inroads into the workings of the community. If you do not assimilate well into their society, things could be very difficult in the future. It can also be difficult to blend different cultures and beliefs. Ethnic cultures are not the only thing to worry about; urban to rural relocating brings differences in behaviors, and even differences in time. Some places work on their own clock, and nothing changes that.

Another concern that you may not be aware of until you are already settled in is who also owns your property. While you may technically be the deed holder, there have been many cases of locals using a piece of land for their wants and needs for a long time before you arrived, possibly generations back! I met a very nice lady who purchased 150 acres of land in Tennessee to grow crops, share her food, and build her group. When she asked the others to help after the food was harvested, few showed up, and those that did left their garbage. When she confronted some hunters on her back property, they literally told her that she may currently live there, but the land had been theirs since the Civil War. Such a situation might be nearly impossible to discover ahead of time, but it is something to look into by asking around the community before you sign the papers. If you have relatives in good community standing in that town, that could go a long way to getting you accepted in some rural or backwoods locales.

There is a romantic notion to moving to that cabin in the woods. It certainly can be done, but even the woods are not what they used to be. These days, the woods are now vacation or even bedroom communities. As a suburban or city dweller, it is easier to relocate to an area that has a similar personality to where you were before. This is something to consider when trying to figure out how much woods you really want.

SUBURBAN RELOCATION

If you decide that perhaps the whole banjo scene is not for you, maybe something a little more suburban will fit the bill. With all the urban sprawl that has happened over the last 30 years, there are plenty of places that were once isolated but now have all the amenities one would like to have. We will dig into the various pros and cons of what it means to live in suburbia later on, from how traffic could affect an evacuation to grid repairs in an emergency. Suffice it to say there are some nice benefits to living outside of a city yet having commercial and emergency services only minutes away.

URBAN RELOCATION

If you prefer the concrete jungle, it does offer some advantages, believe it or not. Many of you are reading this horrified at the thought of being caught in the gridlock of an urban collapse. Fear not: There is actually a precedent for this. Urban areas, by nature, attract a wider range of skills and talent that are not always available in more remote areas. There are more options for medical care, housing, food, mechanical services, access to transportation, and usually better funded emergency management.

While the city may offer easier access and more solutions to your needs, there are a lot of potential pitfalls to living deep in an urban environment. Depending on the threat profile and target value of a particular city, high impact events such as gang violence, organized crime, civil unrest, corruption, terrorism, a nuclear attack, a radiological attack, mass migration, and containment come to mind. Containment is what the federal government does when a contagion is discovered in an area. The key to living in an urban environment is to keep a feeling for what is happening at all times and be ready to evacuate accordingly. Even if it is just to another part of the city.

SURVIVAL PLANNING

There are two general types of survival planning, stationary or mobile, and there are pros and cons to both. Since you are

thinking of a retreat location I could assume that you are looking for a place to hunker down, but that would be a poor assumption.

Many people these days are open to the idea of having choices in survival. This means they might want to purchase pieces of property in various locations and move a camper or RV around as needed.

Others prefer the stability of putting down roots and having a real structure to prepare according to their desires. A property that you can modify and maintain allows you to design a site plan, build at your leisure, and know it inside and out. A more nomadic existence requires organization, planning, resourcefulness, and the uncertainty of security since you are not there all the time. Campers are a nice, affordable way to take home with you but they don't always hold up to the wear and tear of long-term living. At some point most of them end up dying in place. But, until then, they are quite enjoyable.

Whichever way you choose to go, the search will be just about the same. If money is a concern and you have time on your side, choosing an empty piece of property and putting a camper on it while you develop the homestead might be a good option. If you need to relocate and maintain a family and regular employment, it may be better to purchase an existing home that meets the most of your needs.

ENVIRONMENT

The three types of community—rural, suburban, and urban—are really just population density choices. Once you figure out how close you want to be to other people and how far you are willing to travel for services, you can decide on the environment that you find appealing. For our purposes, environment will be a broad term to include terrain, climate and elevation, and culture.

TERRAIN

Terrain works together with the climate because the elevations of terrain will affect how the weather behaves. Generally speaking, land temperature changes more quickly than ocean temperatures. As the Earth rotates, the surface friction of the air mass moves air across different surface temperatures and terrain features, such as flat deserts, elevated plains, mountains, and large water features. Even cities, with all of their hot asphalt and concrete, can affect the weather. Some places are positioned in such a way they have unique weather, such as lake-effect snow or tornado alleys.

CLIMATE AND ELEVATION

When choosing where you may want to live, it would be important to look into the climatological conditions that are common

to that area. Your type of survival preparedness will be in part dictated by the local climate conditions.

Climate changes depending on latitude and altitude. The further north or south of the equator you go, the more winter you will have because of the angle of the sun throughout the year. The closer to the equator you go, you will generally see warmer, more tropical environments. When you are considering a relocation for survival, you need to think in terms of what climate would be most appealing, and also what would be well-suited for your nutrition support through bioavailibility.

Temperature. Do you prefer warm sometimes, warm all the time, cool, cold all the time, or cold sometimes?

Rainy or sunny conditions. Do you prefer tropical rain patterns, Pacific Northwest rain conditions, Spring Plains rain conditions, or dry desert conditions? Precipitation also includes snow and ice, and obviously, those will increase as you move north. Precipitation is important because much of survival is conducted outdoors, food is generally grown outdoors, and

your shelter is always exposed to the weather. Additionally, your energy needs increase in colder environments and hot environments.

Elevation. Do you like low lands, flat land, plains, sea level, coastal areas, desert, rolling hills, or mountains? All of these offer rural, suburban, and urban centers.

CULTURE

Culture has a wide-ranging definition and can change from one community to the next. If you are not able or interested in assimilating into or accepting the prevailing culture in an area, you will likely feel isolated and find it challenging to network in a way that long-term survival requires.

Think about what cultures you are interested in. Northern border, northeast, nautical, Midwestern, Southern, Deep South, Western, Pacific, beach life, swamp life, or farm life? There are countless combinations of these, but if you say them out loud, you will be able to better identify what you want from an area. Family responsibilities may dictate where you go this time, but that is not to say you can't start planning for your big escape in the future.

CHAPTER 4

PURCHASING AN EXISTING HOME

FIND A GOOD REALTOR

A lot of people may ask, "Do I even need a Realtor?" With the rise in popularity of sites like Zillow and Trulia, you may think that you can find a house online and do all the negotiating yourself.

In my experience, for the vast majority of people, this isn't realistic. Buying a home or property these days is not like it used to be. There are all kinds of regulations, red tape, lending and titling issues, and not to mention, are you knowledgeable in that local market? A good, experienced agent will be a major time-saver and offer a wealth of knowledge that will come in handy when you need to make some tactical decisions along the way. If your agent doesn't seem to be acting in your best interest, find another one. You are not bound to anyone until you sign an agreement, but once you do sign, you will usually get much better service since they know you are serious.

BUDGET AND FINANCES

A good rule to buying a new car is to not test drive anything you cannot afford. The same applies to shopping for a new place to live. You must keep your expectations in check. If you look at something out of your budget and fall in love with it, you will find it hard to settle for something more sensible. I have seen a lot of families insist their budget is firm and then get emotionally or unrealistically detached from the line in the sand that they originally set for themselves. You may find a mortgage broker who will fit you into a loan, but with no wiggle room in your finances, you could find yourself evicted from the place you designed to protect you from all the bad things.

SPRUCE UP YOUR CREDIT

Before you start shopping for places to live, tune up your credit report. You may need to delay a move until your debt is paid down and your score goes up. Be patient; it will pay off and you will be in better shape to afford what you want in a home. There are plenty of credit reporting and repair options available. Apply the old adage of "spend more time managing your money than spending it," and you will be in a better financial position. If you need to take some time to get ready, look at it as an opportunity to do some more research. Besides, if you are actively working on your plan, you will be more likely to keep up the discipline to tune up your finances.

PREQUALIFY FOR A LOAN

Take the time to get prequalified for a loan if you are going to need one. This will give you more strength in negotiations and you will know exactly what you can/should spend. Keep in mind that just because you qualify for a loan value, using the full value may not be in your best interest.

CHOOSE A MORTGAGE

Everyone's financial situation is different, but when purchasing property, you have some options. Mortgages these days are wildly unpredictable and the underwriting process as of this writing is very cumbersome due to the economy and post-recession regulation.

Fixed-Rate Mortgage vs Adjustable-Rate Mortgage (ARM)

As of the time of this writing, mortgage rates are at a historic low. However, as with all financial decisions, the rates can change at any time. For some people, the stability of having a fixed-rate mortgage is appealing because you know what your monthly payment is going to be...for the next 30 years or so. For other people, getting a super-low rate right now is more advantageous, and they figure they'll worry about the increased rate in the future, if/when it happens. A popular ARM is a 5/1, where the interest rate is fixed for the first five years, and then changes every year after that. Do you want to worry what your payments will be in the future, or do you want to sacrifice later and enjoy a minimum payment now? These are questions you will have to ask yourself. Run the numbers with your family and your mortgage broker to determine which is best for you.

FHA Loans

The Federal Housing Administration (FHA) mortgage insurance program is managed by the Department of Housing and Urban Development. Typically, most people think that you have to be a first-time home buyer in order to use this type of loan, but that is not the case. Check with your broker to see if this option is available to you. The upside to this type of mortgage is that there are very low down payment requirements, making the amount that you have to pay upfront significantly less than the traditional 20 percent. However, the flipside to this type of mortgage is that you will have to purchase mortgage insurance on the loan, which may increase your monthly mortgage payment by several hundred dollars a month. As with all things, there's a trade-off involved with this program, so make sure that you understand the numbers before you sign on the dotted line.

VA Loans

If you are an honorably discharged veteran, you have the benefit of using a VA loan. This will help you avoid a high down payment, so use it if you can. You earned it. I cannot stress this enough: If you are using a VA loan, use a lender who has proven experience with VA loans. If you use an inexperienced lender, it can hold up the entire process and cause major headaches. It could even cause you to lose the opportunity on the home you want. Make them prove they understand the process and ask for references. VA loans are a great benefit and they are not at all difficult to use, but they have some additional requirements that a lender will need to satisfy.

One of the biggest favors you can do for yourself is to request your Certificate of Eligibility (COE) before you even begin to look at properties. Go to the US Department of Veterans Affairs website and find information on the Certificate of Eligibility under Home Loans to learn all the requirements for requesting your COE. You will indeed need your DD Form 214, or honorable discharge form, for all things VA, so have it handy and never, ever let the original copy out of your hands. It is a challenge to replace.

Another note on VA loans: If you have a service connected disability, you may be eligible to have your loan funding fee waived or even refunded in the future if you eventually become classified as disabled. This can mean thousands of dollars back to you.

USDA/RHS Loans

The US Department of Agriculture offers a loan program for certain properties based on their location and classification as "rural." Pros: The program is similar to the FHA program, in that you have a smaller down payment. Cons: This is a limited program, as it only applies to very specific areas of the country, and there are also income limits. The borrower's income must be no more than 115 percent of the adjusted Area Median Income, which also varies based on location.

FACTOR IN ADDITIONAL COSTS

There are a lot of costs involved in buying a home that you might not realize, including closing costs, inspection costs, title work and other legal costs, potential repair costs, moving costs, property taxes, income taxes in the new area, utility startup deposits, vehicle registrations and licensing in the new community, escrow dollars, insurance premiums, and various travel expenses. There may also be homeowner association (HOA) fees if you are so inclined to expose yourself to such tyranny.

WISDOM TIP

If you are moving from a state that has no income taxes, such as Florida, to a state that does collect income tax, be sure to know what this will cost based on your expected salary. This could be a significant amount that you did not think about. At the end of the day, the dollars only go so far, and if you move from a familiar monthly budget to one that's new, you need to stay on top of it.

Depending on the month you move into your new home, the HOA may require a deposit or prorated payment. Be sure to ask for this information as part of your due diligence so there are no surprises. Sometimes these up-front costs are already paid for by the seller, so it is worth checking through your agent and on the seller's disclosure.

These days, banks want a hefty down payment based on the purchase price of the property. Just be careful to not bite off more financial burden than you can chew in hard economic times down the road. If your job doesn't pan out, income checks bounce, or you face a major medical crisis in the family, you will still be on the hook for that mortgage payment. You'll also want to furnish or fortify your new retreat, and that costs money. Once you crunch the numbers and come up with a comfortable home shopping budget, keep this number in mind and stand by it. During the months prior to actually applying for a mortgage, do not make any major purchases or change employment, and be sure to pay your bills on time to remain qualified.

MOVING LOGISTICS

Regardless of whether you are moving across the street or across the country, you will have expenses that are out of the ordinary. A move of any real distance is a bigger challenge for several reasons. First, you need to travel back and forth to physically visit and see the properties, leading to expenses from travel to food to lodging. (Prepare to eat out; cooking never seems fun during a move.) If you need to take time off from work, this could also be costly, so you'll need to plan accordingly.

Once you have closed the deal on your new place, there will be moving expenses to consider that most people never think about.

WISDOM TIP

Remember, if you want to take it with you, you will in some way pay the cost to move it. Some items may not be worth paying to move and some may be better to sell, donate, or toss and replace later. I know you have been saving that antique yak harness just in case the grid goes down and you need to plow a field, but do you even have a yak? I bet there is a Cracker Barrel restaurant manager out there somewhere saying to himself, "If only we had an old yak harness to hang on that wall..." I'm just sayin', let it go.

If you need to move more than you can fit in your vehicle, you may need to look at a moving service or at least a do-it-yourself option.

Most moving services charge based on the space you need to hold all of your stuff. For example, if you rent a truck and drive it yourself, you pay for the size of truck you need and the miles you drive. If you pay for a pod-style cube, you rent the number of cubes you need. If you pay to use a semi-trailer that you load yourself, you pay by the foot of trailer space you use, with a minimum. I've found that using a freight company trailer that you load yourself is the most economical for large loads. One such company is U-Pack, which is a division of ABF Freight.

It works like this: The freight company drops off a semi-trailer at your place, and you get three days to fill it up as you like (weekends don't count against you). The trailer is marked in one-foot increments and is nine feet tall. You play Tetris with all of your stuff and fill it up as much as you want. When you have it loaded, you place a bulkhead separator that they provide and call for a pick up. A truck and driver arrive and they make note of how much trailer you've used. The driver locks the trailer, and off it goes to your new home. Nothing more for you to worry about. If the trailer is not full, they may use the rest of the space for commercial cargo, but never for other personal loads. This keeps the cost to you much lower than renting a big truck and driving for several days.

If you're moving extremely heavy equipment, such as a gun safe, additional fridges/freezers, or generators, make sure that you have a way to lift these items! Consider getting a moving truck with a lift gate, or bite the bullet and hire movers.

On the other end of the move, you can call out some local help to unload the same way. When planning for this kind of help, do not wait until the last minute, and remember that the end of the month is when everyone seems to need help moving, so availability will be limited and prices higher. These are some

WISDOM TIP

While you can go all over town and collect boxes for free, investing in a bulk purchase of boxes from any standard retailer, like U-Haul, Home Depot, WalMart, or Amazon, saves time and money. And because they come in several standard sizes, they stack much better than all those odd sizes and colors you find in dumpsters covered in meat juice. Who has time to dumpster dive during a move? You can go online and order the boxes to be delivered or prepared for pickup at your local store, too. Additionally, if you keep the receipt you can return the unused boxes for a full refund. While you are buying boxes, don't forget rolls of shrink-wrap, bubble wrap, packing tape, lifting straps, and a good-quality hand truck/dolly or two. You can always sell the hand truck online if you do not want to keep it later.

of the unexpected expenses we talked about earlier, but some things are worth it.

WISDOM TIP

You can save some packing money by using paper to wrap fragile objects. We used a lot of leftover blueprints from construction jobs and it worked great. Also, be sure to write in bold, heavy permanent marker what is generally in each box and which room it needs to be sent to when you get to the new house, or you will have a mountain of boxes with no idea what goes where and what is in each one.

Just keep in mind that expenses will come up and the farther ahead you begin the planning process, the better suited you will be to make a smooth move.

All of this information may seem off topic for survival, but keep in mind that at the heart of survival is the need to be organized and make effective use of time, resources, and materials. Regardless of whether you are trying to survive a plane crash in a jungle or move your family from one location to another, you are always better off with a well-considered plan of action. After that, all you need to do is work the plan and make adjustments as needed along the way.

NONTRADITIONAL SALES

AS-IS PROPERTY

As-is means exactly what it sounds like. What you see is what you get. You also get what you may not see. There are no warranties, usually no negotiated repairs, and no help later. When a property is sold as-is, there is usually something wonky about it, or the owner just wants out and over with it for any number of reasons. If you decide to look at one of these, think long and hard, ask questions, and buyer beware. Also, try not to overestimate your personal DIY/repair skills. This can ultimately cost you big money in the long run.

PRIVATE SALE

Another sale to be aware of is the "for sale by the owner" type. Private sales can also include family deals. Keep in mind that money is involved, and where there is money, there is always the potential for trouble when things go wrong. If you are doing a family or friend deal, be sure to take all the same precautions you would with strangers. This keeps everything on the up and up and out in the open. A misunderstanding can divide the closest family, and you do not want that here, a retreat location that everyone knows about.

Ask your Realtor about these nontraditional types of sale and they may tell you that the owner just doesn't like to pay a Realtor a fee to sell his house. This may be true. It also could be that there is something wrong with the home and it cannot sell through traditional channels. Again, buyer beware on nontraditional sales like a private sale.

CASH-ONLY

While there are many consumer protections in place, cash-only deals will sometimes still have problems pop up that can be costly. When purchasing with cash, it is imperative to research what documents need to be legally signed and recorded. Take all legal precautions that are available. Often, there is little to no recourse for defective or failing home components, and once you hand over the cash, you lose all of your leverage for anything that has not been properly recorded, repaired, replaced, or requested.

From the moment you pay, be sure to always have in hand all proper ownership documents, titles, deeds, rights, permissions, and anything else that is essential to prove your ownership, regardless of whether the arrangement is with friends, family, or complete strangers.

No one wants to hear it, but for all real estate translations, it is actually a good idea to reach out to a real estate attorney just to be safe. Especially on nontraditional deals. There are many pitfalls to buying property but they can be easily mitigated if you do your due diligence and keep in mind these are business transactions. There will be plenty of time later to turn your transaction into a home...or secret survival lair.

HOUSE SIZE VERSUS LAND SIZE

In many developing areas, there are usually two choices for the average homebuyer: small, or older, homes with larger lots, or larger, newer homes with smaller lots. It just seems that finding a house and property that meet both land and house size expectations can be harder than expected. This is especially true in areas that are economically growing and thriving. Most people will need to compromise on the land-versus-living space dilemma. This is where you must hold onto reality and not get emotionally distracted. Know your budget and family's requirements, and stick to them.

In a recent study, one of the top regrets homebuyers reported was not buying a big enough home. Of course, this was not always an oversight; in many cases, buyers were unable to afford the house they wanted. It is not unusual for a buyer to choose a home that may be the right size yet needs some tender, loving care. The thinking here is they can take some time to do renovations later. This can certainly be accomplished as long as you have a complete understanding of what you are getting yourself into.

If you want to take on a fixer-upper, then get a solid home inspection to help you decide. Some places really are a money pit. They may have been glorious back in the day, but today they will drain your resources just to bring up them to code, meet current design trends, or keep the elements at bay.

When you begin your search, start with the size of the living space you need first. Your home will be your shelter. Then,

HIDDEN SQUARE FOOTAGE

During your internet search of listings, keep in mind that houses with basements and converted attics may not list the additional square footage of these spaces because they were not permitted and thus not taxed. If they are not in the building department/tax database as permitted living space, the real estate agent who prepares the listing may not know about it. Agents do not physically measure rooms for listings; they pull public information from municipal databases.

You can often find a 2,500-square-foot house with a finished or unfinished basement, easily bringing up the livable space to over 3,500 square feet. When setting your online search parameters on a real estate website, plan your search for a lower square footage and list a basement as a feature you want to find these deals. Better yet, if searching online, enter a square footage of zero because many real estate agents do not include the square footage in the description. This tactic will reveal houses that would otherwise be excluded in search results. This is a handy trick to include properties that otherwise might not populate your search.

consider the size of the property. Most of your time will be spent indoors, anyway. It is actually easier to find the right house with an agreeable lot size than it is to find a lot with the perfect home. In Chapter 1, you learned that homes in rural areas where the neighbors are separated can be in danger of violent and sustained crime. Homes that are closer together, where you can yell out to your neighbors, are less likely to fall victim to "duration attacks" because neighbors may see something out of the ordinary and say something. If you are looking for a group property, then the isolated rural option may be a great fit. If you are a small, unconnected family, you may benefit from neighborhood collaboration. This doesn't mean you have to tell everyone about your plans, but build relationships that will pay off in times of distress.

Ask yourself if the size of the property you have in mind is practical. Many survival-minded families seem to default to the romantic notion of a ranch with a thousand acres of usable farming and hunting land. Those places are available for a price. Such a place would be a great retreat location if you can manage it. If it looks good to you, it will probably look good to anyone else that is familiar with it or stumbles across it in their travels. A large property is a nice buffer, but will you ever need to defend it? Will it appear to transients as a good place to set up camp if they must evacuate the city? These are things to keep in the back of your mind.

There are some property features that may be worth considering if they are available, such as water features, forested areas, terrain features, caves, or abundant wildlife. Some larger properties that come up in your search may have infrastructure already in place, and that adds value. Some things to look for that can simplify the whole search process would be onsite or nearby grid power, water wells, structures, fencing, food-growing potential, etc. A decent-size property for a family or small group could be as little as a few acres, as long as the land is usable. We will explain how to determine what this means later on.

When it comes to house size, be careful in your thinking. A couple of empty nesters may be fine downsizing to a 1,100-square-foot cracker-style home, but if all the kids and grandkids arrive with their families, space will be at a premium. If you want harmony at the retreat, be careful not to cram everyone together, or it won't be long before there is mutiny. The old saying that putting a wife and a mother-in-law in the same house is like putting two cats in a pillowcase is very true. As a rule of thumb, an active family of four generally requires around 1,500 square feet of living space, not counting a garage. This falls on the lower end, depending on ages and activity levels. Ideally, 2,500 square feet would be better suited for such a family and allow for growth. Once you start adding supplies and equipment to the mix, you might find that you really need a house in the 3,000-square-foot range, or more. Of course, don't forget to take into account any basement or outbuilding spaces that can offset storage needs.

You might look at hundreds of homes and properties online during your search for the right place to purchase. At first you might have an idea of what you want, but usually that ends up changing somewhat by the time you see what is out there and what prices are running.

WALK-THROUGH CONSIDERATIONS

As you visit homes and properties in person, there are many things to take into consideration. I will assume that if you are looking at a property, you have already decided that the neighborhood and surrounding community meets your needs.

If you like the home, you have much to do in a short time because this might be the only time you actually get to walk through it before you place an offer. A good Realtor will be patient with you, but their time is valuable, and the level of service you get will improve if you are considerate. This initial walk-through should only take 10 to 15 minutes at the most. You are making a big purchase and considering this area as a possible safe place for your family, so look at this trip as an intel-gathering mission to get a feel for the human terrain as well as the physical terrain. Much of the intel-gathering process comes from little bits of random information that are compiled to create a bigger picture.

- **Scrutinize the neighborhood as you arrive.** The drive into the neighborhood will reveal clues such as how old the homes are and how well they have held up to the elements. You will also get an idea of the type of people who live around the home. For instance, are the surrounding yards well kept? Is there any indication of the type and price point of the vehicles in the driveways? Is the general landscape and vegetation lining the streets mature, or does it look like it was planted within the last couple of years? What is the condition of the hardscape? Are the roads well maintained?

- **Survey the surrounding homes for clues about the neighbors.** These would be your direct neighbors, those nearest to you on either side, behind, and across the street. Do they keep things tidy? Too tidy? Do they have barking dogs? Are they renters? Do they seem to get a lot of visitors? Is there any evidence they like to party noisily? Are they just creepy? There are a list of things you may not want to deal with, so you may as well take a peek over the fences.

- **Take note of the home's curb appeal.** First, it is an investment and you may want to resell it someday. Second, you are trying to determine if the asking price is reasonable to you. Third, outward appearance has a direct connection to your security planning, as I will present to you later.

- **As you walk up to the house, examine the construction.** Is anything in obvious disrepair? Do you see any wood rot at the front of the home? (Look closely at window frames around the sills and roof fascia boards.)

WISDOM TIP

When you drive up to a property, you will experience a range of emotions from "absolutely not, no way will I live here" to "maybe" to "I kind of like it" to "wow, this is awesome!" If you decide to step inside, you will need to check those feelings at the door and remember that this is a mission to find the right property for the right price that will suit your needs. Emotions can trip you up and there is too much to do right now. Do not allow yourself to build in a bias for this house until you check it out. If you allow such a bias, you might find yourself ignoring things that need costly repair. You may need to remind yourself that this is first and foremost an expensive investment and you already have a hard budget number in mind that you need to stick to.

- **Make a mental map of the house's layout as you walk through.** Layout is more important than square footage. This is an important point to understand.

- **Take a quick tour through the rooms one floor at a time.** Do this to get a sense of whether or not this is a place you want to look at more closely. Do not get distracted by staging or the owner's belongings. If this is not the house for you, cut your trip short and move on to the next property.

If this is a house you would actually consider buying, begin to take a closer look. As you take another spin through the rooms, investigate for clues of any trouble, strange construction, wonky layout, or anything off-putting.

- Are the bedrooms in good arrangement? This means are you comfortable with the proximity of the bedrooms to each other. If you are planning to have children, would you want the master bedroom on the main floor and the nursery upstairs where you would be walking up and down several times a night with baby bottles? Would you want them closer so you can keep an eye on them? Would you want the kids' rooms directly next to your room with thin walls?

- Is there enough closet space, storage space, and basement space?

- How many bedrooms are there compared to bathrooms? How many vanities are in the secondary bathroom if it serves multiple bedrooms? How many people will regularly use that bathroom? Some houses have three secondary bedrooms, each using one common hall bathroom that has one sink. If you have kids, you know this is not an ideal situation.

- Take a look out of each window to see the surroundings. This is important for nuisance reasons but also for survival security reasons I will discuss later on. Nuisances would include neighboring windows, noises, highways, playgrounds, sports fields, barking dogs, and an air conditioner or pump near the bedroom window. Other nuisances include bright street lights on poles or a neighbor's ultra-bright yard flood light aimed at your bed or couch.

- What is the general condition of the flooring?
- How is the fit and finish of the home? Are the details such as drywall and woodwork tended to, or was anything done sloppily?
- Take a quick spin through the yard and look at the house from outside, as well as the yard/property layout.

If you are still interested in this home after this initial pass, go through the house again as if it is a serious investment, because it is. You can save yourself major expenses and headaches by determining in advance how much time, money, and energy this place will take.

Your Realtor can be very helpful in guiding you responsibly through the selection process. He or she should not sugarcoat anything and should be honest and tell you if a home is a money pit. With that said, if you want a fixer-upper, by all means, your Realtor should be happy to assist.

Here are some of the key home systems to look at when seriously considering a home during the initial walk-through. This part may take up to an hour, so keep moving and don't get distracted. If you start to see too many needed upgrades or repairs at this point you can either make note, or choose to let this house go and move on in the interest of time.

Once again, don't let emotion convince you that this is the house for you when your wallet is dragging you back to the car to leave.

Exterior Features

Roof: Check for age, wear, and obvious damage.

- How many layers of existing shingles are present?
- Is there roof flashing? Are there water diverters? Is there proper clearance of siding from the shingles to prevent wicking?

Gutter condition: Check for proper flow toward the downspouts.

- Are there any obvious gutter leaks causing wood rot?
- Are the gutter spouts directed well away from the foundation to prevent water erosion or intrusion into home?

Exterior woodwork: Check for rot, insect damage, and weather damage.

Windows: Check for type, condition, operation, single or double pane, and any signs of moisture between glass layers or around the window frames. Pull the curtains aside to see the walls under each window.

Siding or stucco: Is there any buckling, cracking, or settling at the second-floor level?

- Are nails popping out from siding?
- What type of siding does the home have? Concrete, vinyl, or composite board? In the South, you may see a lot of stucco.
- Are there any signs of the siding swelling, indicating moisture wicking from the bottom?

Exterior paint: Has the siding been regularly painted?

Foundation: Are there any wall cracks, indicating settling? If so, are there any signs that the cracks are increasing in size? All concrete cracks; that is usually okay, but if the crack shows signs of expanding, you may have an active settling issue that could get expensive to repair. Check for these red flags:

- Any signs of serious erosion around the foundation?
- Any signs of mold, smells of dampness, or rotting of wood or drywall?
- Any visible signs of water stains on walls or ceilings, new or old?
- Any misalignment of doors, swelling of wood, or doors not latching correctly could indicate the building is racked (settling or suffering from wind damage). Any windows binding also indicate a crooked structure.

Chimney: Check to see if there is a cap present, or if the flashing is rusted or displaced.

Wood deck: Pay attention to the condition and age, whether there is proper rail attachment, or spindle placement to prevent children from getting stuck or falling through. Are the steps in good condition? Are there handrails at all surfaces that are elevated?

System Features

HVAC: Look at age, operation, and efficiency rating.

Water heater: Review age, condition, venting (if gas), and temperature-pressure relief valve with unobstructed pipe to floor or piped to outside of home.

- Check the water softening system's condition and age, if applicable.

Electrical system: Review age, style, and amperage size of the electrical panel. Is there any room in the panel for additional breakers if needed? Additionally, check for:

- Any signs of previous do-it-yourself work that may not be to code or any hazardous conditions, particularly concerning the electrical and plumbing systems.
- Any signs of electrical arcing in the panel, wiring, or at any outlets.
- Ground fault circuit interrupters (GFCIs) for all outlets located near water and outside in the weather? (Current standards look for GFCIs in kitchens, bathrooms, garages, and near sinks and exteriors outlets.)

Plumbing: Is there a well system? Is there a septic tank and drain field system? When was it last pumped out?

Pool: Check for obvious cracks, and pay attention to pump condition and age.

- If the pool is inground, does it look like it is cracking around the deck surface?
- Is there a pool safety fence?

Interior Features

Check the fireplace for interior sooting and its damper operation. Will the kitchen require renovation in the next 10 years or sooner? Will the bathrooms?

Will major appliances likely need to be replaced in the next few years?

If there is a basement, are there any signs of water intrusion or flooding?

Is there a garage? How large is it? What is the door condition? How close is the garage to the kitchen? This is important when unloading groceries.

Are there any signs of infestation or insect/termite damage? Look for soft baseboards and evidence of black or tan powdery piles around wood.

Are there any signs of other damage, such as repairs to drywall or recent painting that might cover up a defect?

Are there any indicators of a previous fire? Does the attic look like all the wood is the same age, with no sign of repairs?

In General

Does anything about this home or property generally stand out, leading you to suspect that it may not be safe or adherent to local building codes?

Is there a seller's disclosure listing anything regarding the structure? You may not get this form yet, but you can request it at this time. A home inspector will look at all of these items and much more.

* * *

Okay, now that you have given this home a serious look, you have some decisions to make. Depending on the market, you may have to move very quickly, or you may have some time to sleep on it. A word of advice: If this is the home you see yourself actually purchasing, you may want to make a move, but keep in mind to not be hasty. Hasty decisions can be very expensive later unless you know what you are doing.

Whatever you choose, there is nothing wrong with making your offer contingent on inspections, which gives you some breathing room to get the house properly inspected. You can always modify your offer later or negotiate with the owner to make some repairs if anything serious pops up in the inspection.

HOME INSPECTIONS

As with everything in survival, there are trade-offs between wants and needs, and purchasing property is no exception. With emergency survival, your currency is usually calories and resources; with home buying, it is pretty similar, but the resources include real dollars.

There are many considerations to keep in mind before buying a livable structure. Obviously, if you buy a home that needs more than a simple coat of paint, that work will cut into your customization fund. This is where knowing your budget is most helpful. You may want to prepare yourself to accept less land or an older home if you are trying to relocate to an up-and-coming community. The challenge associated with older homes is the cost of customization. But prior to customization, making it livable also costs money.

The age of the building is going to make a difference. The newer the home, the more it will cost. As you look for homes, you may find the perfect house for the perfect price. All of a sudden, you can't believe your luck, and then you realize that the home is 12 to 18 years old (or more) and has the original roof and appliances. This is about the average length of time for replacement for a shingle roof or durable appliances of that era. These days, the planned obsolescence of durable goods has dropped from 20 years to as little as 3 to 7 years.

Also, bear in mind that older homes were not designed with today's energy costs in mind. That beautiful Craftsman home with the fantastic yard sounds great until you realize that the old, single-pane glass windows will cost between $5,000 and $15,000 to replace. If you choose not to replace them, your heating and cooling costs will skyrocket. That perfect home you found may need a roof in the next couple of years, and that could cost between $10,000 and $25,000, depending on the roof size, materials, and building codes in the area. There is nothing wrong with calling for a quick, ballpark quote from a contractor to help you calculate how much a repair could cost.

To get a solid opinion of the condition of your prospective new home, hire a local, well-recommended home inspector. They are well worth the cost and could easily save you from the nightmare of buying, and then being stuck with, someone else's money pit. They will check all the home systems and general condition of the structure. When they are done, you will receive a comprehensive written report complete with pictures and maintenance recommendations for your specific components. This report almost always is completed within 24 hours or less. A great inspector will also be glad to walk you through the entire house and explain all of his findings and offer answers to all of your questions. It is recommended that you, as the buyer, be there for the inspection if possible.

While some states might have a home inspection as part of the disclosure package, not all states have this requirement; only a few states have any regulations for inspector certification or licensing. Most home inspections are done at the request of the potential buyer, and the seller is not privy to the report unless the buyer offers to reveal it. Inspections need to be performed as early in the due diligence period as possible to allow time for any contractor estimates to be received before the deadline so purchase negotiations can be accurately conducted. There is a cost for a home inspection, so don't hire an inspector until you are very serious about a particular property. A home inspection report is a valuable negotiating tool and very helpful in calculating the cost of repairing and replacing key home systems. Don't take the fingers-crossed approach, you know, where you're hoping everything is fine and assuming that the previous owner was completely trustworthy.

Also, a home inspection may reveal things that the current owner isn't even aware of yet, like a roof issue or an electrical outlet they haven't looked at in 20 years. For example, a common roof issue includes defective asphalt shingles. There is such a shingle that exists on thousands of homes and often the seller doesn't even know about it. The problem is when sometime down the road you go to file a claim for some damage only to find out the material is not covered due to the recall. The insurance adjuster will eventually find this out and deny the claim. The new homeowner would be stuck for an entire reroof out of pocket. A typical reroof can easily cost $10,000 to $25,000 for a single-family home. Remember, if you buy it, and it's broken, it's still yours.

Even with an inspector, there are some limitations, and they should clearly define those limitations in writing for you. A good home inspector will never offer his or her opinion on the expected life of a particular structural component or appliance, but they will let you know the existing condition and the average lifespan of a component. You will need to work toward an informed decision from there.

Home inspectors will also not be able to test certain home systems or appliances in some cases. For example, though most home inspectors test the air-conditioning units, in the winter, the thermostat may not register high enough temperatures to let the unit turn on without damage to the unit. The ambient air temperature needs to be at least 65°F for an air conditioner to be tested; otherwise, they can be severely damaged. If purchasing a home when the temperature is too cold for a proper inspection of the cooling system, it would be wise to ask for a seller warranty or have a qualified HVAC technician perform an additional evaluation of the system. The opposite may be true when attempting to test a furnace in the summer months.

The same can be said for utilities; if the water, gas, or electricity is turned off, the inspector cannot test anything that's connected to water, gas, or electric. If the home has been winterized and there is no water in the plumbing, the inspector cannot test the toilets, sinks, dishwasher, or other plumbing. This is logical, and something you will want to take into account during your property search.

If you hire a home inspector, be sure to look for a reputable and experienced company. Ask your real estate agent for a recommendation and call a couple of inspectors to inquire about their service, just as you would do with any contractor. When the time comes for the inspection, make sure that the seller has turned on all the utilities so everything can be inspected. You do not want the inspector to arrive and not be able to test a home component, such as the plumbing, simply because the water is shut off. The inspector will not turn it on and will not find an open pipe in a wall, which could flood the house.

Home inspectors will never cite building codes against a home feature because of the variables in different communities. Every community operates under different building codes because of the process to accept the new code releases. Sometimes it is political, sometimes it is financial, but regardless, they are always different. The home inspector would be overstepping their responsibility and expose themselves to legal action in the future.

A home inspector is an extremely valuable resource, but if something comes up during the inspection that may be a concern, you would benefit from asking a licensed contractor that specializes in that trade to provide an estimate. In some cases, there may be a small charge for the service call, but at least you will get a diagnosis, and they will usually offer their opinion on life expectancy and replacement costs. As a point of consideration, an inspector should not be the contractor, and a contractor should not be the home inspector. This presents a conflict of interest. A good home inspector is a neutral, independent third party and should act as such by presenting a complete, unbiased inspection report.

So you may be asking yourself, why spend so much time on the home inspection? This book is about SURVIVAL. At the end of the day, you're buying a home for you and your family, and my job is to help prevent you from making a huge mistake in purchasing a property that may not be right for you. In prepping for a survival situation, you want to make sure that your time and money goes toward your supplies/training, not fixing roof shingles or anything else that might be part of basic home ownership. It is better to know ahead of time if something is near the end of its useful life or if there is a serious structural concern that must be addressed. Do not get emotionally attached to a money pit unless you have the finances to pour in. Another parting thought on this: If all the comparable home prices in the area are the same or lower than what you will put into this home, you may never recover that investment. And you may come to realize that your ultimate survival retreat is actually...somewhere else.

TO BUY OR NOT TO BUY

You may find a good-sounding deal on that fixer-upper, and if you are handy, that could work out great. But if you are not handy you will need to pay to have all the work done. Will the home be worth the additional expense if you decide later on that you'd like to sell? If the answer is no, it may be wise to let it go and keep searching for another home. This is not limited to just homes, either, as I will present shortly, as the property itself could require far too much in terms of sitework and infrastructure to be a viable option for many people.

Since you will be looking at multiple homes and properties, work as a team with your spouse and agent to take notes and remember things about the house later, helping you decide which home to buy. After a while, they all start to blur together, so it's okay to take notes and perhaps even some pictures if you get permission.

You may be wondering, why all this talk of resell values in a survival retreat? Even though you may be planning for long-term survival, it is wise to consider the resell potential of the home throughout the process. Just because you are preparing as if this is your last retreat, the apocalypse might not happen on your timeline. You may end up selling or passing the property down to family at some point in the future. It is still a major investment and it's best to know what all of your options are for down the road.

WISDOM TIP

At the time of this writing, the housing market for existing homes is hot for properly priced stock. If the house has been on the market for a while, you may want to take a moment and figure out why. A good Realtor will know immediately what is going on if he or she is in tune with the market and the community, and is knowledgeable with home construction.

CHAPTER 5

CAN YOU MAKE IT HERE?

The realities of starting over will come down hard on the family if you have not taken the time to consider how you'll survive in this new location. There will be changes, and just like going to work at a new company, in about 30 days you will begin to see things you didn't see before, some good, some bad. If your family lives in the heat of south Florida or Texas and you want to relocate to Montana, you may get a rude awakening as winter sets in. If you worked outdoors in the warmth and do not have skills that will transfer to indoor work in the great white north, this will be a shock when you can't feel your fingers. These challenges can be overcome, but you need to have a clear understanding of the area you are moving to. Different areas of the country can be drastically different when it comes to climate, terrain, insects, wildlife, length of days, and, yes, people.

People will always be your biggest problem in any situation, especially a highly charged survival scenario. You can think your way out of almost any situation until another person is involved, and then your survival can become a moving target as the situation constantly evolves, requiring you to adapt and improvise.

If you are from the South and are used to people being friendly, when you move to the big city up north, the culture may take some getting used to. The opposite is also true. These considerations are not just for you but everyone in the family.

If you are not sure, delay your move and visit the area to get a feel for it during seasonal weather extremes. Start looking at the kind of employment opportunities listed on job websites, and read the local news to see what happens in the community. Do a search on Google Maps for the goings-on in the communities you are interested in moving to. Check out the school ratings online. Call a couple of Realtors and ask questions that concern you. Of course, they want to sell you a house, so don't take the opinion of just one person.

As you begin to identify areas of interest, you will want to think about safety considerations, such as the crime rate. There are online crime statistics you can find about an area with a simple search. While you are at it, look for the police and sheriff departments on Google Maps; the results will have review rankings, just like businesses. Another search would be for fire department statistics, such as average response times, locations of firehouses, and your proximity to the municipal jurisdiction line, which may affect your response time. This may be a deal breaker for buying a property, but it is good to know for preparedness purposes.

As you refine what it is you want from a selected area, look deeper into what it has to offer. A family with kids will want to know the distance to schools. Also, check the school ratings and compare your public and/or private school options. What is the level of medical/trauma care? Where is the nearest landfill? People have made the mistake of buying a property only to later discover that the county dump is about a mile upwind.

GATHERING INTEL

When you get serious about a property, proximity to threats and hazards will factor into your decision to purchase property. Part of your due diligence should be to take advantage of local source intel.

Ask a long-time resident. Nothing will tell you more about an area than an elderly, long-time resident. Ask and they will tell you what the high-water mark was for that flood you never heard about, that leaky pipeline that was hushed over, and who the bad apples in the neighborhood might be. A note of information on real estate agents: They are legally not allowed to answer certain questions regarding demographics or other opinion-based questions. Real estate agents are bound by the Fair Housing Act, and if they violate the law with respect to forming opinions based on race density, for example, they could lose their license.

Stop by the local emergency operations center or the main firehouse. Let them know you are thinking about buying property locally. They will happily reveal a book full of hazards and plans for how they respond to each. These will range from extreme weather to that old dam out by the lake that will wash out your evac road and maybe flood an entire community. They will identify chemical plants, railroads, and highway hazmat emergency concerns. Most of these plans are not secret; they want the residents to be partners in safety. The only plans they will not share are those regarding protection of critical infrastructure from terrorism and attack. They won't even tell you what is considered critical infrastructure out of an abundance of security these days.

Visit the police department. This should get you information on criminal activity in general, but again, no specifics. Keep in mind that policing is directly tethered to politics, and you may not always hear the whole story on law-enforcement operations.

Visit a local library. If the community is historic (old), they may not have digitized everything for a web search. Old newspapers, books, and local blogs may be of assistance in your search.

In addition to these sources, drive around the area and look for things of concern. Think terrain in the winter, flooding potential in the spring, gridlocked roadways at any time, and proximity to other community liabilities. Other considerations would be less of a threat, but that annual apple harvest that sends thousands into your country neighborhood for several weeks could gridlock your small roads, which can turn your commute into a headache.

WISDOM TIP

It seems that everyone has an opinion on the best place to bug out or set up your retreat. Many of these thoughts are valid, but here is the thing, where do *you* want to be? Is there a family need driving you to move? This is your move, and it may not end up where someone else says is ideal, but it doesn't have to. It just needs to work for you.

MAP RECON

Google Maps is an essential resource. In addition to aerial/area recon, you can use it for map recon. If you are concerned about your search history, go into your Google account settings, turn off history, and set your web browser to incognito or private. When you wish to drive to an area privately, make sure your Google location history is turned off from all phones traveling with you. If it is turned on, you can open your location history and see every single place you have been, how long you were there, how many flights you've taken, and where and when you've taken them, including information from years previously. Also consider turning off all GPS family tracking apps if you are concerned. It will be nearly impossible to avoid all tracking history unless you leave all phones at home and walk. Most cars are somehow also connected to the net these days.

Here's how you can use Google Maps to create your own battle map of all resources, assets, and community liabilities:

- Sign in to a Gmail account.
- Open Google Maps.
- Click on the menu, indicated by three lines next to the search bar.
- You will see a sidebar tab that says "Your Places." Click that.
- Now you will see four tabs. The last one says "Maps." After you click here you will see a window that says "Create Map" at the bottom.

This will give you a map that you can search and save points of interest for anything you want. It is easy to get started; for example, search for hospitals and they will pop up as green pins. (You can edit the color and icon easily.) Keep in mind that these are searches, and hospitals are also called medical centers. You may want to add urgent care and any other types of medical service that is of interest to you. Zoom into any area you want and search again. It may take a couple of searches to get everything to show up.

When you are searching for the best community to live in, think about your proximity to services. If the airport is important to you, a home two hours away may not be right for your situation.

If you or a family member needs specialized medical care, the distance to the doctor may be a concern. If you run a small business and your customers or business resources are inconveniently distant, that could cut into your profits and response time. The same is true for the quality and availability of employees. The further away from town you are, the less choice you have in employees. Shipping has vastly improved over time but if you live too far off the beaten path, you may pay more to send and receive materials. Do these searches for anything you think is important. Here is a list of keywords to get you started (note: you can also use the organizational heads as a search term):

Sanitation

- Landfills
- Recycling centers
- Waste management
- Garbage service

Shopping

- Grocery stores
- Supermarkets
- Malls
- Liquor stores
- Brand-name hardware stores

Law enforcement

- Corrections department
- Jails and prisons
- Police departments
- Sheriff
- FBI
- State patrol
- Penitentiaries
- Detention centers

Transportation

- Train stations
- Bus stations

- Airports
- Airfields
- Railroads
- Bridges

Emergency services

- Fire stations
- Fire departments
- Ambulances
- Paramedics

Power and industry

- Nuclear plants
- Chemical plants
- Biohazards
- Dams
- Mills
- Electrical and hydroelectrical plants
- Other industries

Health services

- Health departments
- Laboratories
- Hospitals
- Medical centers
- Specialty clinics
- Urgent care services

Government offices

- Centers for Disease Control
- Veterans administration offices/medical centers

Military

- National Guard Armory
- US Army posts
- US Navy
- US Marines
- Air Force base

- Weapons depot, maintenance depot, train depot, etc.
- Training grounds
- Military reserve locations

Education

- Public and private schools
- Universities
- Community colleges
- Childcare services

Other public services

- Post office/parcel shipping centers
- Public works
- Electric company
- Libraries

Once you have plotted all of your points of interest, you can save the map to refer to at any time. This will help you get a feeling for the community around any address you want to enter. By knowing the proximity to something hazardous or an area known to have jails or even assets such as hospitals, you can make informed decisions about a property.

To go a step further, turn on the satellite view and look at the area to see into other yards and dense areas that you would not see while driving. The content may not be fresh, but you will get a feel for the area. If the area is far away, turn on street view and "drive" down the road to see what the street-level view is. This is helpful to see the terrain elevations from the ground and the view from the road of different properties. Keep in mind, the tree cover visibility will change at different times of the year in areas where there are seasons. The maps will also help you get an accurate commute time (see Commute Traffic Conditions on page 101), distance to various places, and best routes to use.

TERRAIN AND ELEVATION

When you are doing your map recon, take the time to look at the terrain. Certain terrain conditions may not be deal breakers when purchasing a property, but if you are thinking of how to best utilize your terrain, think in terms of elevation.

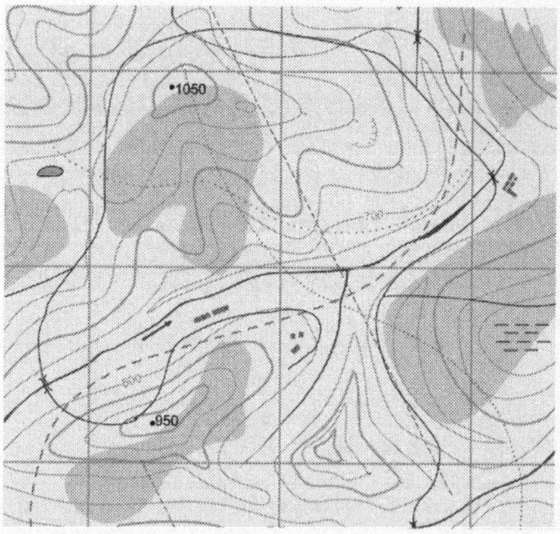

Topographic map

Historically there are two beneficial elevations: high ground and level ground. High ground gives many advantages, such as the ability to observe distances. It is easier to fight downhill, and it tends to be less likely to flood. High ground can also work against you when it comes to observation. Silhouetting can make you visible against the sky, and hilltops are easily located as a reference on maps. High ground may not have easy access to water, either. You will need to have a plan to acquire clean water. When considering high ground, take the time to consider the angle of slope you may be exposed to. Water, rocks, trees, and everything else above you can be a hazard if it breaks loose and rolls downhill. If sloped terrain becomes saturated, you could even be threatened by a mudslide.

Level ground, on the other hand, is the best for building and farming. It provides advantages for building construction. If you are purchasing property that seems too good to be true, it may be in a poor building location, such as on the side of a mountain. This are would require significant site development to make the property buildable. Take care to consider the usable flat space available on a property.

Sloping properties are common, but thought should be given to issues like erosion, water runoff, maintenance, mowing, and room for outdoor activities.

There is a topographic setting on Google Maps that will identify terrain elevations. Use this to identify if you are unknowingly buying a place in a flood plain or other natural hazard zone. If you see creeks or other water features, you can assume those are the lower elevations where water is headed or collecting. The areas downstream of a lake or dam often have higher flood potential than those above the lake. Areas where a river has a sharp bend or flatlands nearby may flood when the river rises. This is also true with any elevated canal systems like the New Orleans Corps of Engineers region. After Hurricane Katrina, the Corps repaired the levies, so outlying area levies are not able to contain the water and new areas now flood.

More recently, a number of catastrophic storms have happened after nearly 10 years of relatively quiet weather. Hurricanes Harvey, Irma, Jose, Maria, and Nate have all stretched the response and recovery systems in challenging ways. When we talk about geography, we also must include islands. At the time of this writing, Puerto Rico is currently in a humanitarian crisis, as are several other Caribbean islands. The storms that hit the coastal and island areas often change the topography in a way that will affect future residents differently. Lakes and other water features can appear where there were none, and the trees and vegetation that held the ground firm may no longer provide that security.

Wildland interface fires have also charred many thousands of acres and thousands of homes and businesses in recent seasons. These fires have changed the terrain by reducing vegetation, causing landslides, and sealing the surface soils in a way that prevents water percolation, leading to hazardous flash floods.

If you wish to dig deeper into terrain types, you can log onto the US Geological Survey (USGS.gov) site and search topographic maps for any area. Study the white or brown contour lines that tell you how abruptly the elevation changes. Close lines indicate a steep drop, and these areas may be prone to wildfires or landslides. Lines that meander apart indicate flat or low lands. These areas may flood. Level lands near a water source may be great for food growing but could also be a flood plain that can be a problem someday. Your homeowners insurance could also be affected by hazard areas, such as flood plains and distance from water sources, or fire hydrants that the fire department may need to use in an emergency.

Elevation will also be a factor in communications. If you intend to use any form of wireless technology to communicate, it can be limited by terrain elevation, natural and structural density, and interference. Wireless radios may say they are capable of 35 miles of range on the package, but this will not happen unless you are on the open ocean on a clear day or talking between hilltops with line of sight. Even then it will be rare to make it work. Most likely, you will be able to communicate over a few hundred yards in most environments.

Elevations also come into play when trying to get terrestrial radio and television signals. If your new place is behind a hill or mountain, you might not get anything on the radio or TV. Many areas with this terrain have not been upgraded with fiber optic cables, which means your internet may be slow. Densely forested and mountain shadow areas can also block satellite TV and internet signals.

Urban areas may have a modernized grid for all things power and information, but if the grid goes offline, your backup plan to use radios could be hampered by all the concrete and steel in the buildings. If you choose to live in the city, work out a communication plan to signal or communicate from high ground before the grid goes down. The same problems can affect any plans to work from a bunker or underground. While you may be well-protected underground, your information and air intake infrastructure will be above ground. You will need to be creative to camouflage these devices from anyone who might happen upon your bunker location. A blast door may be capable of withstanding a nuclear detonation, but it does not take much to put a trash bag over your air intake until you open the door voluntarily.

TATTLETALE TREES

If you are concerned about visibility, certain areas of forest are seasonal, and the trees local to these areas will shed their leaves in the fall. The two types of tree you will usually encounter are coniferous and deciduous. Coniferous trees are simply needle- and cone-bearing trees, such as pines. Deciduous trees are leafy, and shed their leaves at the end of the growing season.

The type of tree you see on your potential home site will tell you a lot about the land you may need to survive on. Deciduous trees create their own compost; the falling leaves convert to nutrients for their roots, and these types of trees indicate good growing soils. They also indicate moist but not usually flood-prone property. Deciduous trees are also usually hardwoods, which are good for cooking, fireplaces, and furniture due to their low resin content. Trees such as oak, hickory, maple, birch, and beech are great for a homestead.

Coniferous trees are good for making common lumber but they are too sappy for fireplaces or smoking meats. Pine needles make a nice vitamin C–rich tea and other herbal remedies, but more importantly, they do tell you that the soil around them is not the best suited for growing. Since they do not have leaves that fall, they do not compost the soil. Usually, they will be in areas that dry out relatively quickly, such as sandy soils. These soils often tend to be acidic and need to be amended in order to grow many types of food.

Cypress, melaleuca, ficus, and banyan trees, which are common in the tropical southern areas of the US, are an easy indicator that the soils in that area flood regularly or stay very wet, such as in swamps or tropical zones. The good news is that when you see these types of trees, you know that the water table is near the surface of the ground, so a fresh water source water is either close by or easy to dig down to.

You do not need to be a tree expert, but it will pay off to know these basics when you are walking a property. You can make an informed decision as to how much work will be needed to fix the soils and for growing, what the flood potential is, how much land clearing you will need to do, and if you can dig an underground structure that won't flood.

SOIL

Soils are more than just dirt. They can be an important factor when considering construction and growing for your new homestead. In construction, there are three general types of soil. These are classified as types A, B, and C. Type A is the most firm (undisturbed clay), type B is disturbed clay or fissured soils, and type C is the least firm (sand). Essentially, this helps you figure out if you can dig a hole without a likely cave-in. As a safety note, the less firm your soil is, the more you will need to shore it up to prevent cave-in or collapse.

While soils can be amended for nutrients to grow food, the type of soil structure can affect many other projects. Sandy soil is not cohesive and will not hold a wall for a hole. Safely digging a hole in different soils requires something called the angle of repose. All this means is, the softer the soil, the wider the hole you need to dig to prevent it from caving in with potentially catastrophic effect, unless you brace it properly with building materials suited for the job. One cubic yard of soil can weigh as much as a car. The Occupational Safety and Health Administration (OSHA) says that any hole deeper than 5 feet must be braced with proper shoring material unless the hole or trench is angled by terracing or steps wider at the top than at the bottom. Do your research to determine the proper benching, bracing, or wall angle, depending on your soil conditions.

If your property is to have defensive positions, such as foxholes, trenches, or bunkers, the type of soils and presence of water will alter how you dig and how you build. If you try to bury a sealed structure underground in a place with a high water table, it will either flood or pop out of the ground. If you are going to bury anything, choose an area that is dry all year and not exposed to surface loads, traffic, or prying eyes.

The type of soil also matters when it comes to your property holding water. Storm runoff coming down a hill or through a creek can flash flood, which can destroy your camp or homestead in a moment if you set up in the wrong place. If you are situated on a muddy plain or sandy creekside, these are indications that water frequents that location.

When choosing an area to settle down, look at the ground for indications of heavy rock formation. You may not be able to plant if the ground is only a few inches of soil on solid rock. In areas where the ground freezes you will have a situation called frost heaving; this means you may be growing rocks as they get pressed to the surface.

If you are buying a piece of land to build a structure, look around for any possible erosion signs. Water runoff can pour into your basement or foundation and cause structural problems later. Mother Nature does not like to be diverted when it comes to water, so take a moment to make sure you can provide a permanent and economical solution to water flow and erosion.

WATER

Water is the source of life. You will need to have it on your property in some fashion. Water is provided in several ways and you can easily find back-up or alternative water sources with a little planning. It is always wise to have more than one source, or at least have a way to store some water, in case the primary source becomes unusable. Many properties have either city-provided water or an on-site well for daily use. We all know the problems of depending on city water, such as contamination potential and failure of the system if a pipe breaks or the grid goes down. A well can be susceptible to the same problems, but alternate power or a manual pump as a backup can mitigate a disruption of supply. If you are on a well or need to dig one at your new site, it is important to know how deep the water actually is. In some places the water is very shallow and in other places you may need to dig an 800-foot well. These are cost considerations for planning your site work if you plan to develop the lot.

Having a surface water feature on the property can be good depending on how easily it can be utilized for the many daily tasks of everyday living. How close is it to the house, the garden, and the animals? Is it running or stagnant? Is there a natural spring on the property? Since water is so important, you will need to have a plan to protect it from contamination and other people who may want to seize it for themselves. A running creek on your lot sounds great and it is nice to have, but if something is dead in the water upstream or a contaminant is leaked into the stream, your source will become unusable. There are also new laws to be aware of that restrict some uses of water on private lands. The good news is that in most areas, water is free from the sky and a good afternoon storm can provide almost a year's worth of supply if you catch and store it well.

With water always comes sewage. When looking at a home or property, ask about how the sewage is handled in the area. In some states, you can build a whole house without a permit but you absolutely need to explain how you are going to dispose of your sewage or risk going to jail. Sanitation is a critical element of survival.

If your potential property has city sewage, try to figure out which way it goes from your house. Does it flow downhill or is it pumped uphill? We all know where waste wants to flow and we don't want to be there when that happens. This includes entire neighborhoods as well as your basement. If the municipal sewage system were to fail, it would be wise to identify a place on your property away from your fresh water source, garden, and livestock to dispose of the human waste. Preferably downwind, if possible. Does your property offer a possible solution to this potential problem?

Waterways such as rivers, canals, and creeks are also a traditional avenue of approach and transportation for people. If you are looking at a location near any navigable water feature, keep in mind that people may be moving around on it. What can they see from that position? Are any of your important items visible?

EVACUATION ROUTES

We cannot always time the need for an evacuation. Even though this may be your last planned place to be, stuff happens. It is wise to give yourself as many travel options as possible. Aim for a minimum of three evacuation routes, and the nearer they are to your new place, the better. You will not be the only people thinking the same thing, so when you get serious about a property, take the time to look at the population density in your area and how your routes could be affected in a mad rush evacuation of the communities along your routes.

WISDOM TIP

If you decide to move into a traffic-monitored area, take the time to set up the cell phone apps and news alert sources for that area and every area along your evac routes as soon as possible to keep you situationally aware from the beginning. Trying to sort this out in the middle of a disaster is just another thing to do and, as with all things tech, it never goes easily when you are in a hurry or preoccupied with something else.

Remember to factor in feeder roads and main travel ways. The daily commute during rush hours will give you a sense of the traffic density. Google Maps or Waze both provide real-time traffic updates. As you hone in on an area you like, take a look at the live traffic maps on Google or Waze at various times of the days to get a feel for the traffic patterns. This is important for evac routing, but it is also a good indicator of your daily commute to work and may save you the headaches of gridlock. Many cities and states now have a web-based live traffic alert system to help you become aware of delays by showing live cameras and real-time incident reports.

When evaluating a property, look for terrain or features that can work both for and against you. An example would be a bridge. Some properties have small bridges on the entry drive. Bridges are essentially choke points, great to keep bad people out because they may be the primary avenue of approach, and they are easy to defend. But that can work both ways. If your bridge is not maintained, it may not hold the weight of a firetruck, or it could wash out in a flash flood. Generally, bridges are a great way to cross ditches, creeks, waterways, and other roads, which are all considered linear obstacles or linear hazards. If you have these linear features on or near your new property, how may this affect you? Positively or negatively?

Roads and creek beds are not the only avenues to be concerned about. Power lines, maintenance easements, railroad tracks, nature trails, forestry firebreaks, fence lines, rivers, and other linear hazards could mean unwanted visitors. These are not deal breakers, but something to think about if you are trying to be invisible to passersby.

Consider, how visible is your property from the air? Drones are becoming commonplace these days and while you cannot do too much about the aerial enthusiast peeking over your trees, you can make an effort to keep your private business out of sight. This is more important if you are located near a potentially hostile area. If times get bad, people will start looking for signs that you might have something of value. Does your new property offer concealment from prying eyes?

TACTICAL LANDSCAPING

Luckily, you can make improvements if the piece of land you fell in love with is lacking in some ways. What would it cost and how

could these improvements be done? Those are fair questions to ask. Another good question is, how long do you have to make improvements based on projected civil troubles? What materials would you need to invest in, and which projects would be highest in priority?

The terrain of your prospective property has even further implications. How might you be able to improve or add to the defensive terrain? If you are concerned about the two-legged animal snooping around on your property, you will want to examine the field of view from your homestead. As you look out the windows of the home, is your view clear or is it obstructed? Having a home tucked away in the shade of trees is a nice thought but the same trees that shade you give cover and concealment to trespassers. Another reason to clear brush and trees away from the home is the hazard of wildfires getting too close. Try to keep at least 30 feet of clear area around the house, if not more.

Part of your security plan should be to see or be warned of people wandering onto your property as much as possible. You may want to consider what it would take to clear the lot of unnecessary brush and items that present blind spots in your view. If there is thick, impassable brush that would channel an intruder into your field of view, you may choose to leave that in place. Such channels reduce the number of places you need to closely watch, which is helpful when manpower for security is limited.

In planning your defense as you scope out a new property, you might consider where fighting positions would need to be placed. These positions will also need clear fields of view (fields of fire). As you remove certain vegetation, you may wish to install what I like to call tactical landscaping. Essentially, this is any plant, bush, vine, or natural obstacle that would inhibit the ability of trespassers to approach your home or get against the house to climb in through a window. Think spiky, entangling, thick, or otherwise deterrent to an intruder. Tactical landscaping creates channels to force the trespasser to go where you want him to go. Ultimately, he should appear right in front of the defensive measure you have waiting for him. Fewer approaches equal fewer places for you to defend.

WISDOM TIP

Apply some basic landscape design measures and use plant height in a way that supports you seeing as much as possible but does not offer the trespasser many choices of cover or concealment. When designing your physical security measures, look outward from every window and door to identify enemy hiding spots, then go outside and pretend to be the enemy. How many ways can you find to sneak up on your house without being seen? Those are the spots you want to address so you can take away the enemy advantage. There are many available books on home landscape available for reference. You may need to use less friendly plants than the books suggest, but the design theory will be very helpful. Usually, xeriscape plants fit the bill pretty well because they require little water and are uncomfortable to crawl through.

Tactical landscaping should be employed based on the mature height of the plants chosen. From low ground cover, plants should reach medium height to tall. Low plants that are effective include cacti or other spiky plants, while medium plants would include roses, azaleas, etc. Tall plants would be berry bushes, vining plants, or dense entangling hedges. For added measure, you can add barbed wire within channeling plants. Water features can be added or improved on as channeling features. For added delay of trespass, you might choose to add fencing across a water feature.

When choosing or building a structure, take a look at the window layout and how far above grade the windowsills are. To prevent intruders from entering through a window, place a thick hedge of sharp or spike-laden plants that presents strong standoff from the window. If you need to evacuate through a window, you can toss out a thick blanket or comforter onto the plant to reduce injury during egress.

To complement the tactical landscaping on your new property, you can install various fencing or man-made material that would make any trespasser very uncomfortable as he takes a knee or lays prone on his approach to the home. Tangle foot wire may be the solution. This is essentially fence wire or barbed wire mounted to stakes in the ground and supported approximately shin height to keep someone from running or walking through an area. It is known as a disrupting obstacle. The key to disrupting an attack on your property is to disrupt the attack plan. Once the plan stalls or trespassers become unable or unwilling to proceed, you have an opportunity to gain the advantage.

These are just some examples of how to look at a piece of property from a defensive or security improvement perspective. Once you unmask the potential of a property, you can begin to calculate the cost benefit of property improvements. Simple physical security measures do not have to be expensive if you are willing to plan and work a little. If such measures are not your concern, you can focus on things more relevant to your property search.

TERRAIN AS PROTECTION

You are looking for a place to go for long-term protection, so it makes sense to consider how to make the land work for you in that respect. Most troublemakers will arrive by foot or vehicle. Very few will arrive by air, but in the new world of cheap drone technology, almost anyone can do a flyover to see what is not visible from the ground. When considering a piece of property based on terrain, high ground is usually the best place to be. Though if your house enjoys a breathtaking view while perched atop a mountain, it is probably visible to others for miles. Visibility is key to security, but the trick is to see them before they see you if you are worried about unwelcome visitors.

Security is a very important consideration in survival. The most effective security is placed in layers and is not too obvious. You probably will not find a property with an acceptable security plan in place, but any property can be quickly graded on its potential for defense by applying the 4-D plan. Whether holing up for the night or creating a long-term retreat, remember these four words: deter, detect, delay, and defend.

- **Deter** = Does the place look like an easy, valuable target? Or does it look so formidable that there must be something worth the risk on the inside?
- **Detect** = If someone were to come here, how close would they get before you saw them?
- **Delay** = If they were to come close, would they be delayed due to the natural terrain or man-made obstacles?
- **Defend** = If they wanted to attack you here, does the land favor you in the defense?

Now that you have analyzed the natural terrain, how much work would it take to improve all the above phases of defense? If the property is strong in several areas and weak in another, you could focus your efforts to improve the one weak area, but if all four areas are weak and costly to improve, this may not be the best place to plan your last stand.

Of course, that is on the extreme end of thinking and not for everyone. These are guidelines, so don't worry if you find yourself closer than you might like to a neighbor. Closely situated homes have the deterrence and detection effect of neighbors looking out for each other. It is beneficial to introduce yourself to the nearest neighbors to get a feel for them. Don't be shy; go knock on the door and take the initiative to say hello, and maybe even get a glance into their personality. This would leave you only to improve the delay and defend parts of your physical security plan.

Another consideration that dovetails into the benefit of terrain is the avenue of approach, more commonly called a road or trail. Any terrain that allows people to approach your position is called an avenue of approach. The fewer approaches a property has, the easier it is to defend. If everything else is too thick to move through, most people will default to the easy route, thus allowing you to detect them earlier. Warning: Seasoned military types will never take the quick and easy route anywhere because they know the dangers in hostile territory. The old saying goes like this: No one ever got a medal for winning a war ahead of schedule or under budget. How many ways can someone approach your new property? What will it take to channel trespassers from the blind spot areas out into the open where you can see them?

While we are on the topic of approaches, let's look at roads. There are essentially three types of roads for the purposes of this discussion: paved, gravel, and dirt. What you need to be aware of is how or if they are maintained by someone else. If not, it will be up to you. Are they susceptible to natural hazards, such as flooding, ice, snow, falling trees, or debris and blockage by others that could limit your ability to travel? Many remote properties are nicely isolated but have roads and driveways that are so steep, they become unusable at times by ice and snow, and are underwater in the spring, or possibly flash flooded and impassable.

ARE THERE UTILITIES OUT HERE?

Too often, people want to rush out and build their dream cabin on a remote piece of property without considering the costs associated with extending the infrastructure to the site. That amazing lot you found has everything you wanted—trees, a creek, a plot to garden, and maybe a great view—but did you notice where the nearest power line is? Did you have to hoof it on foot for the final hundred yards to reach the perfect home site on the property? Were you expecting water and a city sewer out there? If none of those utilities were present, you probably won't have high-speed internet, or maybe even a cell phone signal.

If you want to be away from it all, this may be the perfect place for you. Just be aware that you will need to make a

substantial investment to prep the site for living, and even building. Construction requires large trucks, and they require solid roads with low-radius bends. Bringing in a prefabricated underground bunker, mobile home, or large roof trusses also necessitates a large truck. Cement trucks do not travel well on steep angle dirt roads, and semitrucks need a lot of turning radius. That winding driveway may be perfect for your jeep but the truckers will curse you and drop their load out on the main drag.

If you are planning to place a large propane tank out there, you may want to check with the gas company first—the gas truck may have limitations on how far their hose can reach your tank. The average bulk fuel delivery truck has maybe 125 feet of fuel hose unless it was trimmed due to wear and tear. Furthermore, the driver is required to see his truck from the tank he is filling for safety reasons. If you plan to place your tank at a distance from the house, plan to pay to bury the gas line the extra distance. Those costs average anywhere from $6–$15 per foot of buried line. If you go this route, factor in the winter months and the ability for delivery on icy or muddy roads to your property.

WISDOM TIP

Yes, you can bury a residential propane tank in the ground. I have personally done this hundreds of times as a licensed contractor, and it is a great idea to keep it out of sight, protected from the elements, and at a lower temperature, which allows another 5 percent of fuel storage due to lower pressure because of lower ambient temperature. Just anchor it properly underground, coat it with a cathodic protection paint, and add a sacrificial anode bag to prevent corrosion from electrolysis due to certain sandy soils or salt water. Also, keep the filler valve accessible in all climates and ground water conditions. Propane tanks have been buried for decades and are still in use today all over the country.

Electrical power lines are going to be a necessity for most homes. If the nearest pole is a mile away, you are looking at paying the electric company to engineer and install the power line and poles for your property. Then they will need to come back and make the drop to your new house. Give the power company a call and ask for a quote. They can usually give you a ballpark cost based on distance. And electricity does not always come straight down the driveway, so they will require you to sign a utility easement over to them if it crosses yours or someone else's property. The same will go for telecom, cable, and data lines.

Another consideration that you will have no control over is the repair time of damaged power lines. If your new property is susceptible to ice storms, hurricanes, or other natural disasters, you will want to know if the property is on a critical circuit. Critical circuits are the lines that get repaired first and usually service critical infrastructure, such as hospitals, jails, police stations, and government buildings. If you are not on one of these circuits, you should plan to create your own electricity for light, heat, air conditioning, refrigeration, and other important needs.

Many municipalities will require some basic services on an occupied lot. Aside from electricity, water and sewer disposal are the most that will be required. In some states, the only thing required is sewage disposal—you may not need a permit to build a house, but you better have an approved plan to dispose of the poo. Sewage can be disposed of onsite by a septic tank and drain field if there is no city sewer, so don't fret if you are too far away from the city system. That being the case, you may also need a well for fresh water. Ideally, you would also have a year-round source of clean surface water nearby. Every lot being different, you will need to check with the county or a local well driller who can give you an idea of how deep you will need to drill on that particular property. You may be able to ask for Geotechs, or geotechnical information, based on soil borings from a builder or developer. This information would reveal the type and thickness of all the soils, as well as the depth of water in the area. This information is useful to well drillers and builders. It's possible, but not likely, that the city will have this information. You might find the information on a previous site building plan if there is one.

Even though water may be reachable easily enough, the water you would want to drink may be hundreds of feet down. This is not the ideal situation for a survival-themed location, but it does not need to be a deal breaker because you can get affordable, alternate-power well pumps as a backup plan.

One last thing on well drilling: In some states, such as Colorado, you can own the surface land but not necessarily the mineral rights, and water is one of those rights that you might not own. You must get approval to drill there because anything underground, including oil, may not be yours to use.

Before you pull the trigger on that awesome lot, ask yourself why it seems so affordable compared to other properties in the area. A great deal on a lot can quickly become a lot of unexpected expenses.

PROXIMITY TO HAZARDS

While flooding is the most common disaster that affects life and property in the US, earthquakes, landslides, wildland-urban interface fires, tornadoes, and storm surges are all events that happen in different geographical locations. While you cannot mitigate every hazard, you can be aware and plan accordingly. Here's an interesting fact: Statistically, the safest place to be in the US is the desert in Nevada. They have the least major disruptive events, and that is why many of the major communications hubs and data storage vaults are located there.

Disaster potential is something to consider, but keep in mind that disasters are not only natural; they can be caused by people. Terror targets can be anything of significant psychological, financial, infrastructural, or disruptive value. When considering a location, take the time to determine the proximity to such places. Crime is always something to consider, and it is not limited to deep urban settings. Bedroom communities may have less violent crime, but they have higher property crime because the burglars strike during the work hours when you are not home.

ASSESSING THE COMMUNITY

The community is a place that can be described as having a benefit to the area, or they might be a detractor. Assets would be places like medical care facilities, grocery or hardware stores, and police and fire departments. Liabilities could be things such as jails, bus or train stations, rundown buildings, or any area where riffraff may congregate. Other potential liabilities could be chemical plants, nuclear plants, railways, or anything that could cause a toxic release. Highways, railways, trails, and utility right-of-ways can be a liability because of the potential for people to walk into your area for many reasons, including disaster and evacuation.

Some places are both asset and liability. You can usually see this when you give it some thought. It may be great to live close to the only store in the area, but what would happen if everyone needed that store at the same time? That could be a dangerous place to be. The same goes for gas stations, pharmacies, and hospitals.

Nuisance features are also great to know before occupying a new home. These would be any place that emits foul smells, such as landfills, factories, water-treatment plants, some restaurants, or places that create smoke. Nuisances can also be sound and light. If you want peace and quiet, moving near a school, daycare, stadium, highway, or railway may be unpleasant. In fact, light pollution is a growing problem everywhere these days. If you want to see the stars at night, locating within miles of a town center, stadium, or commercial facility will make seeing stars at night much more difficult.

The same asset/liability classifications can be placed on your new neighbors and immediate neighborhood. Some neighbors could be amazing and some will be absolutely miserable to deal with. You will not know until you move in.

Moving beyond the property, what does the surrounding community have to offer? Is there convenient medical response and care? What is the law enforcement situation? Are there enough police, and is there any obvious history of problems with the community and law enforcement? Is the fire department regularly staffed or is it a volunteer system? This can affect the available resources and response time in the area. What are the shopping options for everyday needs, and how far away are they? Are there nearby gas stations? Do they have backup power generation to keep the pumps running?

A part of the relocation process that can easily be overlooked is the all-around culture of the area. There are several subsets of a community that can make or break your experience. These relate to religion, ethnicity, socioeconomics, population density, and other various demographics that you may be interested in. Unless you are moving into an area that you are already familiar with, it can be difficult to figure this out. You will just have to ride around and look for the key indicators of the community.

Every community has its bad side of town, if you will, and some communities do a great job of hiding it.

If you are wondering about how the economy is for an area, look at the type of disposable-income businesses (i.e., the quality of restaurants, pawn shops, check-cashing businesses, rent-to-own stores, and dollar stores). Are there a lot of "pay here" style car dealerships, or are the car lots brand name? If many of the buildings in a certain area have bars on the windows and/or graffiti on the walls, that may be a clue to consider. Unfortunately, these days, drug manufacturing and use has moved into suburban and rural areas, making it more difficult to identify trouble spots. You will need to ask around and do some research about grow houses and meth labs, if this concerns you. It is pretty easy to get the inside scoop on troubled areas just by approaching an officer or two and asking. They want partnership with citizens and are usually happy to give you some clues of areas to avoid.

The dirty little secret of law enforcement is that they know the criminals will do bad things. The best the police can do is work to push the crime off to neighboring counties or jurisdictions by establishing a reputation for making crime more difficult in the home jurisdiction, and that is done with citizens' help. It is not unfair to say that the closer you are to a metro area, the more criminal activity, such as property crimes, becomes common. Gangs like to target the suburbs and bedroom communities, too. Most people think crime is done in the dark, but in housing areas, the most burglaries are done between 10 a.m. and 2 p.m., when fewer people are home.

If you are curious for more demographic information, you can do a search for restaurants in an area and see if there is an abundance of any particular type. This can be an indicator of a particular ethnic population. A web search or drive past the churches in the area can also be informational if you are so inclined, but you need to be cautious about judging the book by its cover when making these kinds of assumptions. These are all just bits of information that you will analyze in order to paint a larger picture. A drive will also help you get a feel for the seasonal activity of an area. Many towns are seasonal and intensely busy at various times of the year, and at others, you can't buy a sandwich because they roll up the sidewalks at 5 p.m. This could have a substantial effect on your income, depending on your business.

Demographics can be indicative of security concerns. Again, take care to avoid assumptions, but if the local economy is such that crime is on the rise, consider how that would affect your family at the new homestead and at the places they would frequent, such as work, school, and elsewhere. High-end communities are not necessarily immune to crime, but the types of crime and policing may be different. A chat with some locals may reveal how things really are in the area, because some of the website resources might include data that stretches across distances in the larger counties and skews the results.

HOW OFF-GRID DO YOU WANT TO BE?

If you are relocating to be self-reliant, the next question to ask yourself is, how off-grid do you want to be? It sounds great to cut the cord and have no utility connections to worry about, but that takes some careful planning and budgeting. Utilities are related to important things, such as physiological needs, convenience, comfort, and sanitation.

Physiological needs are anything that supports life and health, such as heating, cooling, nutrition, etc.

In 1943, psychologist Abraham Maslow wrote a paper on the hierarchy of human needs (image below). He believed that humans have five levels of needs that have to be met in order to survive and develop. The most basic of needs are physiological and continue with safety, love/belonging, esteem, and self-actualization. While most everyone wants to feel self-esteem and love, we must tend to our most basic of needs first. Those are the needs that keep us above room temperature. If you are freezing to death, feelings of belonging and self-esteem don't really matter at the moment. So if you want to go off-grid, address just the things that will keep you alive first and work from there toward comfort and convenience desires.

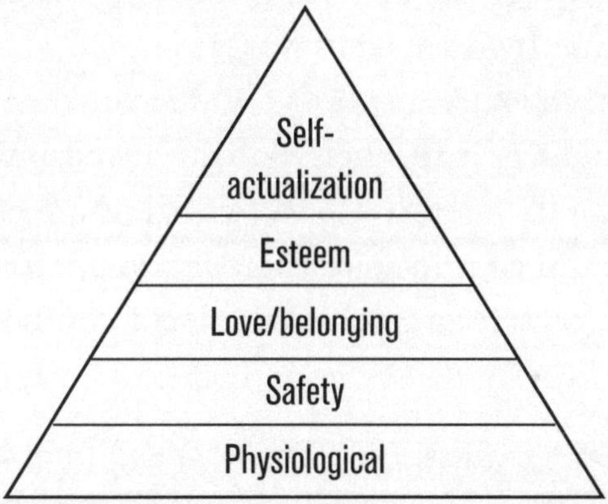

Common off-grid solutions will address electrical, water, sewer, communications, food production, bartering, and various medical approaches. When it comes to off-grid planning, there are multiple options within each of the primary categories. While it does fall outside of the scope of this book to identify every option, the survivor will want to identify a combination of options that will serve best, based on the climate, location, terrain, simplicity, and affordability. Most people begin with some form of energy production and water harvesting. It will be almost impossible to find the perfect off-grid retreat that checks off all your boxes, so keep your mind open for that gem of a property that offers most of what you want, then examine if it can be reasonably upgraded to your desires. A major fixer-upper may divert too much money from your preparedness plans.

EMPLOYMENT/BUSINESS CONSIDERATIONS

Most of us must maintain gainful employment even after a relocation. When you first decided to pick up and move, you probably wondered how you would make a living, unless you are comfortably retiring. There are never any guarantees as to employment, and what you imagine happening may be nothing more than positive thinking. If you need to work, you will need to figure out what the options are in any area in which you desire to move. Go back to your budget. How much do you have to work with now, and how much will you have to work with after you get settled? If you have chosen a rural relocation and your job does not allow you to relocate or telecommute, what will you be able to do for money?

Begin by narrowing down the areas you would like to live in and then researching what kind of work is available. Finding a job in an area that you will not reside in for some months or years in the future will be challenging, but you can do an area search on the internet to see what type of major industries as well as supporting industries are located in the area. Is the area industrial, manufacturing, tech, or service-based? Is the area a seasonal, tourist-based economy? Are you able to offer any services that support these industries? Is your plan to just buy a food truck and see what happens? Who knows, you may have hidden talents as a mobile BBQ pitmaster.

However you look at it, you will want to carefully consider not only your employment but your spouse's as well. Ideally, you would relocate with the ability to live off one income in case something goes wrong. Again, know your budget and make that red line in the sand. Many people these days have the option to work from home or telecommute. If this is you, a low-speed internet connection might be a deal breaker. Ask the local carrier about service. Some houses are just outside of an upgraded server block. Satellite internet is always a possibility, but it is not as fast as a dedicated fiber optic cable in the street.

COMMUTE TRAFFIC CONDITIONS

Another consideration to remote living is daily commute. If you live in a quaint bedroom community along with twenty thousand of your closest neighbors between you and your office, the little, two-lane road you must use can be a parking lot during average rush hours. It is not unusual for your 20-minute commute to be an hour or more if things get bad on the road. I recommend checking real-time, local traffic conditions using Google Maps to get a feel for traffic patterns as you refine your search for the

perfect location to live. Do this for several weeks and at different times of day. If it looks like downtown Atlanta, where the roads are solid red for all but 20 minutes a day, that's a clue. If you see small red spots, zoom in and you will probably see those are just stoplights where people are queued in line. Google Maps will also present you with three route options when you enter a starting address and destination. Each route will display a projected travel time. These times are relatively accurate and often based on real-time traffic conditions.

WISDOM TIP

If there is a road incident, Google will automatically present you with alternate routing in real time while you are driving. I find that this alternate routing may take you off the highway and down a lot of side streets, which seems all kinds of wrong, but in the end it works out to be faster than sitting on a limited-access highway just waiting to move again. This works well in the bigger cities. Naturally, you will want to use common sense when puttering through some sketchy urban neighborhoods. Keep your situational awareness up and running at all times, but rest assured that if Google sent you this way due to road congestion, it sent a bunch of other people the same way for the same reason, so you'll be in good company.

The next consideration you may want to think about is what would happen if you lost a job. If you banked on the employment you had when you moved in and something did not work out, do you have a reliable backup plan for another job? The best plans can fail regardless of your efforts. If you bought the perfect house but must now drive two hours for a position that will pay well enough, you are going to be stuck. Do not get emotionally connected to a house that could become a debt prison.

CHAPTER 6

BUILDING OR RENOVATING YOUR SURVIVAL RETREAT

If you find a home or property that you really like but just feel as if there is not enough space for your purposes, you may be able to make adjustments to the property that could offset this.

MAKE IT BIGGER

It always seems so easy on TV: Just tear out something you don't like and change it (cue the eye roll). An option to increase your structural space is to find a property with an outbuilding, such as a detached garage or workshop. If the property you really want does not have the space you need, you may be able to construct an addition or outbuilding. Keeping in mind the return on investment you'll receive from property improvement, there are a number of options you can choose from to fit your needs, from steel buildings to room additions to underground bunkers to off-site storage lockers. When calculating the space you need, ask yourself if you really need all the stuff you have. Are you willing to pay real money to buy, build, or rent the space to keep it all?

If you consider a property based on the idea of adding rooms or outbuildings, be sure to check if the lot is allowed to add a structure. Do you need permits? What are the required setbacks from the property lines? (A setback is the distance you are required to keep clear from property lines and easements, set by the local building and code enforcement authority.) You can call the local building department and ask what those distances are for your area. They range from zero to about 10 or 15 feet, and sometimes, you can request a variance for special consideration. Before you shrug your shoulders and thumb your nose at the rules, keep in mind that the code enforcers use aerial imagery these days to compare map overlays to see who has built a structure without a permit and without the proper taxation.

If you do not want revenue agents poking around on your property, keep your affairs in order. Anyone who has ever seen a TV show on remodeling may have noticed a recurring theme: The more walls that are opened up, the more problems are found, and the higher the cost of repairs. The hidden problems are always the ones that must take precedence over the desired upgrades because they are usually important, like hazardous wiring, water-damaged structures, leaky pipes, or mold. Of the many renovations I have managed, approximately 50 percent had some amount of mold in the walls that no one knew about—yet. There are approximately 200 different species of mold that can be found in a home, and while only a few are toxic, they are all indicative of a warm, damp environment. The wall cavities of a home should not be damp, so this means something else is going on and needs to be corrected.

STRUCTURAL UPGRADES AND LAYOUT

Construction in different areas of the country varies substantially. Buildings are constructed based on local building practices and accepted building codes. Those codes are created based on several criteria. Most often, construction is regulated based on natural disaster potential. In the United States, we have the potential for just about every type of natural disaster there is. Flooding and water damage are the most common. Fires, earth movement, tornadoes, sinkholes, lightning, and extreme winds are the usual catalysts for building codes. When you decide on an area to relocate, you will most likely be restricted in the type of construction you can use. You can always exceed but never shortcut the accepted building code.

If you decide to have a house built on your own or on a developer's property, there is nothing wrong with that, but there are some

things to keep in mind. Costs for construction are determined by square footage (square foot construction), which directly relates to your budget. I have found this to cost anywhere from $95 to $125 per square foot for the conditioned living space of a new home. Garages cost less due to the more spartan interiors. If you are located in some of the more expensive cities, this price will certainly increase. The converse may apply for certain rural areas with lower prices, but probably not by too much. Rural areas usually have less construction and therefore fewer conveniently located, qualified construction personnel and material suppliers, so you may not get the discount you imagine.

If you are uninitiated about new construction, be aware that the price of the house does not always include the lot. Actually, some builders do not handle lots at all. You may need to secure your property and then commission a builder. Builders are businesses, and this means that time is money.

There are several different ways to approach a new construction build as a homeowner: buy a completed spec house, begin a spec house from the ground up, commission a design build, or take the owner-builder approach. The term "spec" means specification. In layman's terms this just means that all the specifications for this house have been decided, presented to various trade contractors for bid, and built as per plan with little to no input from the future homeowner. Package homes, such as log cabins or manufactured homes (trailers), are another possibility.

Home buying is one thing, and home building is another altogether. When you buy an existing home, you are essentially trying to decide if someone else's home will work for you with as little repair and renovation as possible. When you open up to the idea of constructing a completely new home, your frame of mind will blossom with ideas of design and potential. Slow down a moment; there are a few cautions to lay out for a successful build.

Let's look at each of the types of project to get a quick understanding of what it means and the general process. Building a new home can be a very rewarding process but challenges and headaches along the way are guaranteed. I began this book talking about managing expectations, which you should continue to do in the construction process.

COMPLETED SPEC HOUSE

A builder has invested in a piece of property either by itself or as a part of a larger development. Think homeowners association because these days, homes are mostly built in tracts with this method. The builder has completed the home based on a set of plans he has preselected that he thinks will sell in that particular area of a community.

If the home is part of a larger development, there may be continued expansion and more homes built. This is usually done in phases. Why is this important to know from a strategic relocation perspective? Resale value. If you are the first home built in a new development of, say, 100 homes to be built, you will not see a significant increase in market value until the development is built out, which could take several years, as people who bought around the Great Recession found out, because new construction collapsed and developments and builders everywhere stalled or went out of business. The strategy is to try to buy a home in a development that is almost built out so you get the lower price but will benefit sooner when no more homes are available in that neighborhood. Of course, if there are more unfinished developments nearby that offer lower prices, nicer homes, or better amenities, that will affect your investment as well.

UNBUILT SPEC HOUSE

Everything I just explained holds true here as well, with the exception of the building process. You choose a development and/or builder who presents you a selection of homes they are prepared to build. The builder also offers you a selection of lots to build on, unless you already have a lot somewhere else. You may be invited to visit constructed models for the offered floorplans to get a feel for how they would be finished. Here is a cautionary point: The models are always dressed up with all of the extras and finished by interior designers. If you want that particular look, you will pay for it.

Just like anything else, the advertised price is the base model. While the builder's model may have fancy countertops and hardwood floors, the base model usually offers plastic laminate tops and vinyl or wood laminate flooring. If you choose to have a home built with this method, you absolutely must be clear on what is included and what changes you are allowed to make, and pay close attention to every step during construction. Most builders offer a process similar to à la carte menu ordering. For example, you may not want a bathtub in the master bathroom, but some builders will insist it must be done for some obscure code enforcement reason. In reality, it certainly can be built with only a shower and no bath, but the plans list the tub and the builder would have to submit a plan revision to the building department, adjust the plumber's contract and the fixture distributor's order, and project manage a change to make sure this change is carried out properly. All of this interferes with the accounting for the project. If the builder is busy, he does not want to mess around with these things, so he makes up a story that he's not allowed to change the plan.

Most builders will offer or allow certain changes that are preapproved. Sometimes there is a charge but not always. The more common changes are flipping floor plans 180 degrees or adjusting room sizes and closet spaces. The builder will probably present you with a list of options and upgrades. This is where they present the new car smell and upsell on options. Be careful, and again, manage your expectations at this point. Your budget is set but that upgraded carpet, soft close cabinet hinges, and commercial-style kitchen range would be awesome. Add $12,000, ka-ching! Later, you may find you can add wall receptacles and prewire for data and smart home technology. Then, you discover that the basic roof is only basic three-tab shingle with a 15-year service life. With this in mind, you decide to do the architectural-dimension shingles with a 25-year service life as an investment so that when the house turns 15, you are not replacing all the appliances and roof in the same period.

Upgrades are not a bad thing, and you will see that some things make perfect sense as an investment. But stick to your budget so that your new home doesn't come to feel like a 30-year wage garnishment.

Don't forget to consider the price of the lot, if it is not included. An especially important reminder is the lot development, or something called site work. Developments include all of this, but if you buy your own lot and hire a builder, you might have to also hire a site work contractor to prepare the lot for construction. This includes clearing, grubbing, grading, drainage, utilities, and possibly slabs and driveways. If you go this route, it will be critical to be involved in the project management and force the communication between any contractor you hire and the builder. The last thing you want in the middle of the project is to hear one guy did not do his part while the other guy says "it's not my job." You will need to create a scope of work for any part of work that is not included in the builder's documented responsibility.

Since most people are not familiar with the building process, it will be very important to hire quality tradesmen who are familiar with your area and community permitting requirements. Ask for referrals and call the referrals. Educate yourself because it is your money, and you will have to live in the house when it is finished. You will also want to verify and receive all original or legally accepted copies of any permits, approvals, warranty documents, lien releases, inspection approvals or rejections, and any other pieces of paper or e-mail that will affect you any time in the future.

It is also a great idea to get at least two independent home inspections on new construction: a framing (pre-drywall) inspection and a final inspection. In my experience as a general contractor and building inspector, a lot of things can get hidden in the walls that will become a problem later.

Don't forget to have the roof inspected, too. I strongly recommend working with an independent inspector who is FAA licensed to fly a high-quality drone. Drones used by competent pilots offer a far better inspection than solely using a pole camera or a ladder to walk on the roof. Any inspector who says otherwise is uninformed. Walking on the roof causes wear and damage and does not allow for viewing over the edges, inside gutters, and on top of chimneys without the risk of falling. Additionally, a good drone inspector will include some aerial images of your surrounding neighborhood, property features, and other things in proximity you may not be aware of, like how close you really are to that highway behind the trees.

Do not pay any significant amount of money up front, no matter what they say. Prior to approving payments or drafts, verify that that portion of the work has been satisfactorily completed. Once you pay for something that is not done or done right, you have lost almost all of the leverage you have to get it corrected. There is also a widely accepted practice available to you called contract retainage. This usually works out to 10 percent of the contract price being taken out of every draw or invoice and held by you, the owner, or whoever is paying the overall bill. Once the project is completed satisfactorily and per contract, the retainage is then released to the contractor in exchange for a document called a final lien release. Keep in mind that this is not personal, it's just good business. If you want to say that to the contractor in your best New York mob voice, go right ahead.

CUSTOM DESIGN BUILD CONSTRUCTION

With this process, you are taking a more involved role than with a spec house. Here you are searching and securing a lot or larger property, dreaming up a home design and layout, and hiring an architect to prepare the plans, or blueprints, as they are commonly called. You will go through several changes and adjustments in planning until you and the architect arrive at the desired vision of the structure you wish to build.

This is where having knowledge of square foot construction we talked about earlier comes in. If you know you have a budget of $250,000 and the square foot construction price in that community is $125/square foot, that 3,500 square foot retreat just priced out at over $430,000, not counting mortgage costs or land. Whether you are building a house, bunker, or detached building, math is math.

Once you have a final design in hand, you can present the project for bid. I recommend multiple bids to find the right contractor. If during the bid process you have trouble with a builder, you can pretty much bet he will be trouble during the construction process. Do not be afraid to keep interviewing until you find the right fit in a builder. Again, it is very important you identify the exact scopes of work for everyone involved. If something seems missing in the back of your mind, address it out loud with everyone involved; these little thoughts indicate an incomplete understanding of how something works, and they will plague you until you address them.

These little mind itches may also be indicative of an actual gap or blind spot that everyone overlooked in their individual work scopes. Ask questions and bring people together as early as possible to coordinate and verify that systems and components will actually work together. Everyone will appreciate the communication and it lets them know you are on top of things and watching everything they do. You cannot have square work if someone is cutting corners.

Be patient and understand that even though you have an approved plan in hand, changes will happen. It may be a necessary structural change or, more likely, a series of adjustments to allow better use of space or routing of a home component that obviously does not fit as construction proceeds.

WISDOM TIP

The visible part of the project is called the fit and finish, and the last 15 percent of construction is usually the most expensive and complicated, relatively speaking. This is why you might see shell builders who offer amazing pricing to build 85 percent of your new home, and you get to finish out the way you like. Sounds great, but in reality, he does the easy part by giving you a shell and leaving you to figure out the rest.

Ultimately, the homeowner is responsible for everything that involves permitting and municipal or government approvals. Be sure to verify that all required contractor permit inspections have been finalized and recorded in the building department's system. Keep all paper copies for your records, and do not release funds until the work has been done and approved by the permitting agency or you may be out of luck. When you apply for a building permit, a list of required sub-permits and inspections is included. If a permit is required for something, for example electrical work, and the electrician does all the work without pulling a permit, you pay him, and you allow the drywall company to close up the walls, you may now have to tear out all the walls and have another electrician pull the permit, verify the work was done properly, get the work inspected, and after you pay a fine, you may be allowed to reinstall all the walls. All at your expense.

OWNER-BUILDER METHOD

This is exactly as it sounds: You build it. This has a combination of everything we just discussed, but instead of hiring a general contractor, you become the GC. In many communities, you as the owner of the property can build on your own, as long as you follow all the same codes and permitting requirements as a regular licensed general contractor. There is some benefit to this process in that you can work at your own pace and hire subcontractors to do whatever you need that you cannot do, and there may be a significant cost savings of possibly 30 to 40 percent in some areas.

There are a few restrictions to what an owner is allowed to do in most areas, and those are called MEPs, or mechanical, electrical, and plumbing. These all require engineer-approved plans and licensed contractors; you can hire them, but in most places you cannot do their work. Sure, you might find a slippery contractor who will pull your permit and let you do the work. For a fee, of course. But some things really are best left to professionals for quality, warranty, cost reasons, and, most of all, safety.

And at the end of the day, if your time is valuable, let them get in and get it done quick rather than messing around with it for a month of Sundays. Being your own contractor can save you money but only if you are organized, capable, have the right equipment, and have the ability to get contractor material pricing. Be prepared to dedicate yourself to the building process because you will absolutely spend a significant amount of time trying to wear all the hats.

WHAT TO BUILD AND WHERE TO LOCATE YOUR HOUSE

Now that you have worked out the possible choices of how involved you can be in the construction process, you can think about materials, design, and location. For the sake of argument, let's say your lot is above the mean high water table. (This eliminates the coastal areas, flood plains, and most of Florida, although I like north and central Florida as a possible location.) You can choose from aboveground, earthen berm, and subterranean styles of construction. Some of the best survival properties have a combination of these (and Florida is not by any measure out of the running for a good location). You have several types of structure available to consider. Remember to always consider security and survivability when making your final choice.

ABOVEGROUND HOUSES

Now think of security and survivability. Most northern homes are built in a process called sticks and bricks. This just means that they are wood framing with insulation, drywall on the inside, and some type of flimsy siding material or a brick veneer on the outside. This is great if you need to kick out a wall to escape a fire, but not so much if you are looking for ballistic survivability. Concrete masonry units (CMU), which is another term for concrete block, is stronger and somewhat less flammable. This is a good structure for high-wind zones and most common in the southern coastal areas. Then there is something called tilt wall, or poured-in-place concrete wall, construction. This is a structure that limits flammability, providing a solid ballistic structure that is both well-insulated and exceptionally strong. An example of this was a home in California that was the only home to survive the Calabasas/Malibu firestorm in 1993 because it had no flammable materials on the exterior and no wall or window coverings that could be affected by the thermal radiation from the surrounding conflagration. A home like this would make an exceptional survival retreat.

Log-style homes or steel buildings are other types of construction. Log homes are very durable, sustainable, and environmentally, sound, and they can be assembled quickly. They are energy efficient and the maintenance is not more involved than conventional construction. Ballistically speaking, log homes are stronger than other basic styles of construction.

Steel buildings are a good economical choice in many cases, as they are commonly fitted to the customer's specifications. They can be made to fit various appearances and interior configurations since they usually do not need interior load bearing walls. Steel buildings can be constructed quickly without much experience at a square foot construction rate that is often less costly than conventional construction. Various exterior cladding or veneer surfaces are available to disguise the steel frame, so these buildings can appear as conventional construction. Due to their thin walls, the steel building does not offer substantial ballistic protection and would be comparable to conventional stud and siding of other homes.

An important component to any home is the roofing material. With various roofing materials, such as standing seam, metal tiles, corrugated metal, concrete tile, and slate stone roof, the homeowner has more options than ever before to create a great building envelope, a term describing a complete barrier to the outdoors. I recommend avoiding a wood or cedar shake roof. Wood shake roofs are not a great choice for a survival retreat location due to their higher cost and more frequent maintenance needs. They also do not handle floating fire embers as well as other materials.

Of course, there is also the underground option for a retreat.

SUBTERRANEAN AND EARTHEN BERM HOUSES

In most areas, aside from those with the high-water tables, the underground or basement component can be an amazing survival resource. Due to the many different floor plans available, a secret basement survival or panic room can be constructed to allow residents to hole up for as long as the air, food, water, and sewage will allow. Your imagination and budget are the only limits to building a basement shelter. See page 127 for more information on basements.

Around the world, the average temperature just a few feet below ground is substantially lower than above ground. This provides a great environment for a root cellar. Root cellars most effective in the northern climates, as the warmer tropical environs are still a little warm for leafy vegetables. This is something to think about if you have an underground structure in mind.

If you are able to utilize the subterrain, you may consider a multiuse tunnel structure. This is a larger project, but tunnels have been utilized throughout history to make a clean getaway or to store valuables and contraband.

Tunnels

There are several types of tunnel, and various materials available to the ambitious survivor. Constructing a tunnel can be a hazardous undertaking, and it is vital that safety precautions be taken. We talked about the types of soil and how they may be cohesive and non-cohesive; this is one of those times that it matters. Common tunnels of any real substance are often made of circular drain pipe. The round shape offers strength in the same way an arch does for a brick wall. If you choose the drain pipe design, large-diameter concrete drain pipe is the strongest, and with the proper coating and joint sealing, it can withstand moisture intrusion. But it must be completely coated, as concrete will weep moisture. A large diameter would be more than 54 inches. Smaller can work, but it becomes challenging to move through. If you are going with this design, consider placing what is called a precast drainage box structure at the far end of the tunnel. This is how storm drains are designed. The box usually has a ladder and a manhole. The iron lids can be heavy but can be exchanged for something lighter. In lieu of concrete, metal, or high density plastic piping can be used if you can find it. The best source for these materials are storm drain suppliers or site development contractors who may have some leftover materials from a big project they may be willing to part with.

Pipe tunnels can extend as long as you want and are tied into the house, usually through the basement wall, if you have one. It is important to note that you must consult an engineer before you cut a hole in your basement foundation wall. The soils around your home are compacted to a specific density to prevent settling, and the foundation is waterproofed during construction.

A tunnel can offer a stealthy escape, an awesome storage area, or a hideout, and some people even use them as underground shooting ranges. Tunnels can even be hidden in the wall of a custom panic room. There are many options for concealing bookcase doors and other hidden entrances.

Underground Bunkers

Tunnels are not the only subterranean option. A complete underground structure or bunker might be the solution you are looking for. These days, the word "bunker" has gotten some negative connotations by the general public and has been associated with the tin foil hat crowd, never mind that foil is actually aluminum and not tin at all. But I digress. Bunkers are as popular and available as ever before; actually, they are not your grand daddy's bunker anymore. Today's bunkers are commonly well-built, comfortable, and well-equipped for extended stays.

While this book is not about the finer details of construction, it would be wise to have a working understanding of basic construction and design components, and things to avoid if possible. A bunker is defined as a reinforced underground structure. There are various methods of construction available for a bunker, such as welded steel, concrete, prefabricated large diameter pipe, and even the more natural, such as a reinforced excavation. This would resemble a mine shaft or root cellar. Caves often make great bunkers and historically have been very popular. In fact, Jesse James had a good run in a cave.

WISDOM TIP

A note on any underground shelter that should be obvious: You are limited in exits and, therefore, escapes. When considering an underground shelter, be aware of the exits and consider where they surface. The entries can be as camouflaged as you like but it is a good idea to have more than one. Preferably a second exit that surfaces out of site of the first in case bad guys decide to set up camp on your lid.

As far as components for a bunker, you will have a few non-negotiable requirements.

The bunker needs to be of design that will not fail under the loads of the surface or compaction of surrounding soils. This means that there should not be any deforming or deflection of the structure for any reason. Even slowly bending walls will affect the anti-corrosion coatings you must apply, thus allowing rust and or electrolysis to happen, leading to all kinds of problems, from leakage to structural failure.

You must protect the entire exterior and interior surfaces of the structure from corrosion. The earth will always consume what we bury, and you will need to work diligently to delay this process. Underground structures are not like those on the surface; you cannot just take a Saturday and repaint the outside. Use the best coatings possible and prep the surfaces properly.

You must seal from water intrusion. This may sound obvious, but if there is water anywhere near the structure, it will find a way in. In some cases, you will need a way to pump water out of and away from the bunker with a sump pump.

You must allow for fresh air entry and circulation. Humans require a consistent, balanced atmosphere. Too much or too little oxygen can be deadly. When calculating the atmospheric needs of an underground structure it is wise to know how many people could be present at any given time. If you are concerned about surface air contamination from chemical or radiological events, there are plenty of automatic and manual filtering and circulation devices available. Keep in mind that one of the easiest ways to get someone to open that blast-hardened door voluntarily is to close off or contaminate their fresh air. It won't do much good to have a fully stocked doomsday bunker that can be sabotaged with a trash bag over the air stack or campfire smoke at the intake. Hide your vents and hatches. The best bunker is the one no one knows about in the first place.

You must have sufficient water for the length of stay and number of people on board. Some bunkers have built-in water wells that run on manual or alternative energy.

You must have some way to manage human waste and garbage. Some bunkers have a way to remove waste, or can even be connected to a septic tank system.

You must plan for safely creating energy. Batteries will not last forever, but ideally, you will not be in there forever, either. Caution: Charging lead acid batteries can give off gases, which could be hazardous in confined spaces.

WISDOM TIP

As an underground space, the bunker may let in contaminants with a specific gravity higher than zero. Any fumes, liquids, flooding, or other hazards present outside could find their way in. Consider and prepare for such. Invisible and odorless fumes are so dangerous that every year, many construction workers perish in subsurface environments with no chance of survival without detectors and breathing equipment. Use easily acquired equipment, such as smoke, carbon monoxide, carbon dioxide, and gas detectors to warn you of dangers. Avoid combination detectors as they may not be placed at the proper elevation for the different types of gases. Smoke rises but carbon monoxide is close to equal as air and CO_2 is heavier than air. Natural gas rises as it is lighter than air but propane settles as it is heavier than air.

You must treat any bunker as a confined space, which means it has the potential for a hazardous atmosphere. This means that car batteries, combustion engines, fires, generators, cleaning chemicals, bleach, paints, acids, gases or vapors, propellants, flammables, combustible materials, and even oxygen (especially oxygen) can be extremely dangerous in such an enclosed space.

Water detectors/alarms might be a good addition if you have underfloor storage. Since water is a low-oxygen environment, as scuba divers might say, we would be prudent to properly manage our associations with it.

Shipping Containers as Bunkers

There has been a resurgence of underground shelter design in recent years and there are examples of all kinds of creative design, from dirt cellars to buried school buses to renovated missile silos. One of the more popular ideas people show interest in is the buried shipping containers, or conex. The idea sounds plausible, and containers can make great office and sleeping quarters with the right renovations, but when it comes to burying a container, this falls outside of their design and load capabilities. This is a touchy subject for people who insist it will work. With the proper reinforcing and coating you may be able to pull it off for a while.

The first problem is that containers are essentially a hardened skeletal frame with sheet metal skirting. They are made to stack under extreme loads, but the sides rarely touch anything. Because of this and the need to keep shipping weights at a minimum, the sides are hardly much more than hard curtains. In fact, a simple bump by truck or tractor will dent or even tear the siding.

Burying a container amplifies the weaknesses in the sides. The sides of the container are not reinforced and have no longitudinal or adequately spaced vertical supports to strengthen the sheet metal. This means that even though the sheet metal is corrugated, it cannot handle inward pressure, and when a structure is buried, properly back filled, and compacted, there will be inward pressure due to the weight of the soils and any moisture. This can be worsen if surface traffic or other loads are present. There has been discussion of using rock baskets and various other soil-reinforcing measures to prevent soil pressures if one is determined to make this work.

Additionally, containers leak when placed in standing water. The doors seal against rain but will not hold up to flooding. The siding is originally protected against corrosion for sea travel but every ding, dent, and scratch can damage this coating. These damages are called holidays, and each one will eventually turn into a rust blister, and subsequently a hole, through the process called electrolysis.

Containers also frequently rust on the top because of ponding (accumulating) water from rain. Underground ponding water will do the same thing if the surface is not thoroughly protected with a cathodic coating. The next place a container eventually fails is where the floor connects with the sheet metal walls.

Quonset-style shelter

Corrosion often begins around the welds and rust takes over until the material dissolves.

The shipping container doors are also problematic; one would need to excavate and create a reinforced vestibule of some sort to facilitate the opening of the doors. This means providing a pit essentially with a walk-in or climb-in access with some way to dissipate any water that may collect while preventing a wall collapse. By the time one goes through all of these expenses and effort, you may as well just build a basement type of structure or use a material designed for such applications, such as large diameter pipes. Again, everything is based on a combination of soil conditions, climate, location, and of course, financial resources.

If a metal underground structure is desired, perhaps an earthen or bermed installation would suffice. In this instance, the container is not completely buried but is properly coated for corrosion, with earth placed around it for physical protection. There will still be pressure on the sides, but not as much due to the lower hydrostatic pressure on the walls. When soils are bermed as opposed to below existing grade, water will percolate away more easily. If this design is considered it would be wise to weld reinforcing materials inside the walls of the conex.

Another design is an arched Quonset-style structure with earth piled up and over the top. This is the classic Cold War backyard bomb-shelter structure. The bermed Quonset hut is a design that was born from the quickly fabricated military structures that popped up all over the world by our military. They were designed using the long-proven method of using arches to support the roofing structure. By adding soils over them, the structures received an additional layer of fortification and required less purchased material. Berming allowed Cold War citizens to work on the cheap and still have a decent chance of survival in case of natural or man-made disasters. Both of these designs are good options, as long as you are okay with an obvious bunker-style structure visible on your property and are permitted to do so by your community. In areas where the water table is high, a surface structure may be one of your few options for a fortified shelter.

WISDOM TIP

A note on public relations as they pertain to the new survivor on the block: Unless you do something to narrate the conversation about who you are and why you are there as a new neighbor, the locals will gladly make up something from thin air. The story they imagine about you is never good, so be proactive in being friendly and as chatty as needed, without sharing any real private information, of course. Your preps are your financial and physical survival resources and no one else's business. It is very easy to start talking about the news, then politics, then giving opinions, and before you know it, you have let all the cats out of the bag about your position on things and the next thing you know, you have shared how many guns you have and are beginning to realize what a mistake you just made when someone makes a comment about your arsenal and how no one needs that many guns.

Public relations is just another way to drive the narrative or message that you want to present. OPSEC is important and a little friendly disinformation or information discipline will go a long way toward keeping your home low on the list of places to break into and will, hopefully, keep you labeled as a quality person and not some survival nut job.

HOME FORTIFICATIONS

The survivor who is purchasing an existing home will rarely find a structure that is well-suited for survival. Most homes are made with aesthetics and basic building codes in mind. If you are concerned about receiving some unwanted ballistic attention from outside, you will need to do some upgrades yourself. Today's high-power firearms will make Swiss cheese out of most exterior walls, and the interior walls have zero chance of offering protection to those in the house. If you are building your own home and you have the resources, ballistic shielding can be added.

Several companies offer these products, and they can install them as well. While it is rare for a home to be ballistically protected, it is not unheard of. Many government or high-value individuals have this done for the added piece of mind. Another option to strengthen windows and doors is to install impact-rated doors and windows. These are most common in coastal areas for hurricane protection, but nothing says you can't use them for home fortification. While they will not stop bullets, they will stop just about anything else a group of marauders can throw at you if they are properly installed.

For the average survivor, it will be a more cost-effective solution to concentrate on specific areas of the home and/or create interior protected evac paths to a safe room or escape route. If your initial plan is to defend from various home envelope openings, such as windows, this can be done by focusing your efforts under and around that window with materials that will absorb or deflect projectiles. Some options for this would be sandbags on the interior and extended several feet on either side of the window. Steel plating or other dense paneling can be used to supplement. The windows can be protected with close weave, heavy mesh, or expanded steel to allow a view to the outside but reduce the incoming tear gas or Molotov cocktail. Plans should still exist to extinguish any incoming incendiary device inside and outside, but in a pinch, anything, including a mattress, can slow down window-crawling intruders.

When fortifying your home, think of the primary reasons you are fortifying. To protect people, to protect supplies, to delay trespassers, to defend the structure, and also to give you time to escape if needed. Break it down by wargaming the scenarios you want to prepare for. If you are concerned about invaders, create a path to your safe space. While many of these ideas are not ideal for everyday living, they can be planned for when you build or buy your new home.

BASEMENTS

Homes with basements have the added advantage of underground protection. Due to the myriad layouts for home basements, the survivor can set aside a very comfortable safe space or panic room. A family of four can be comfortable in small panic room for hours or even days with the necessary supplies. Many of today's basements are even stubbed for bathroom plumbing. A well-hidden and stocked bathroom underground could be a great thing. Sewage is always a limiting factor for hiding undetected. Keep in mind that many basements have macerator or ejector pumps to lift the sewage up to the street level sewage pipes, so if the power is off, that could limit the toilet use, but otherwise, it would be great.

Many basements are also designed as daylight basements. This means they are usually surrounded by earth on three sides and a wall with windows or doors to the outside. With this design, there is less chance of being trapped underground in case of fire. Homes with daylight basements are usually found on streets with sloping terrain. The homes on the downhill side of the street will have the basement and homes on the uphill side are usually built on a slab without a basement. There may be exceptions in older construction, as some homes have dark basements with no doors to the outside unless it is an exterior storm door with steps to the surface.

While unfinished basements are like a blank canvas to the imaginative remodeler, you will want to consider how the design will affect the home's resale value. Every neighborhood has a common square foot resale value that is based on an average for the area. Basements are great spaces, but since about half of the potential real estate market doesn't care if they have a basement or not, a built-out basement averages about 50 percent return on investment of the local market square foot resale value. This just means that if the average square foot resale for a home is

WISDOM TIP

Some basements are unfinished, which means they are raw construction with only bare wall studs, little to no electrical or plumbing, and probably no HVAC. This allows the survivor to create many design options, from additional living space to man cave, home theater, or even underground lair complete with preloaded bug-out vehicle to drive out on a moment's notice.

$100 per square foot in that locale, you might get $50 per square foot for a basement that is built out. So if you spend more than $50 per square foot on your basement man cave/secret lair, you might not get that money back when you go to sell.

This loss would especially be true if you build something so niche or custom that you think is awesome but the majority of buyers would try to figure out how much it will cost to tear it all out and do something different.

When selecting a home with a basement, consider the options to drive from the road to the basement door. Is there vehicle access? Is the basement door a single or double door, or even better, a garage door? Can adjustments be made to accommodate vehicles and gear storage? If there is no practical way to drive your bug-out vehicle to the basement entrance, you will probably end up carrying the supplies and equipment either up the stairs or outside the house and around to the vehicle. Often there is either a fence or a significant slope in the yard that may prevent you from driving to the basement doorway. This may not be a deal breaker, but it could be labor intensive when loading out to evacuate or stocking your basement.

WISDOM TIP

Homes with drive-under basements are great for keeping a vehicle close to your supplies, but you do lose significant useful storage space with this layout. You may have to decide between having a drive-under or a larger usable living/storage space. Additionally, drive-under garages usually mean that the car is on a different level than the kitchen, and all the groceries will have to be carried up a flight of stairs as opposed to a street-level garage, where the common layout is a garage on the same level and close to the kitchen. Once you are settled in, you will find that you need to load into the kitchen more often than into a basement in daily family operations.

Any space you wish to utilize will face the same constraints, from basements to apartments to underground bunkers. If your storage space is not conveniently located in terms of your vehicle, you will need more time to move supplies. That's another reason to keep situationally aware and begin the load-out process as early as possible to give you time to complete all of your tasks in an emergency.

Most survivalists prefer to keep their planning and supplies close to the vest. When building or shopping for the right survival home, try to think of where you will put all that stuff you don't want others to see or know about. The general rule is that you will always need more space than you imagine.

The other way to look at survival is to have less stuff and more skills. While there are plenty of items you will need, there are plenty more that you do not need. An old saying is that *stuff owns you*. This is very true. The more you have, the more you need to move around, store, care for, maintain, and spend money on. By thinning out the fluff in your supplies, and the rest of your home for that matter, you can use your ingenuity and resourcefulness to overcome any shortages.

For those who plan to move to a place with neighbors, you can get much further by networking, befriending others, and participating in neighborhood activities than hoarding those boxes of old junk clogging up your garage. If you take the approach of being the new guy with all the cool stuff who keeps to himself, the neighbors will test you to see what you are all about. Especially neighbors who have been in that area as a tight-knit group of friends for a long time. Don't be surprised if there is a knock at your door sometime to borrow something or to ask you to help in some way. They may be testing you to see what your personality is and if you will be welcomed into the local fold. First impressions are important in life, but for survival planning, they are critical.

If you turn them away or isolate yourself, they may do the same when you need help some day. There are strategies to appear to own little of value but be a great neighbor that make a lot of sense. This works especially well in small town or rural areas. Something to keep in mind as you consider these areas for a new home. If you are not a neighborly kind of person, perhaps the hills are not for you.

LOOKS SHOULD BE DECEIVING

When fortifying or upgrading your property, take into consideration the appearance of what you are doing. The more your property looks fortified or secured, the more inviting it becomes to prying eyes. The thinking is that if you are securing something, you must have something of value to secure. Of course, if your house looks like an easy target, that is also bad.

When it comes to the remote cabin in the hills or the isolated farmhouse that you rarely visit, those remote areas may be secret as far as you are concerned, but you can bet the locals already know all about it. You do not know what happened there before you bought it or who is familiar with the inner workings of the house and surrounding property.

It would be a terrible thing to return after several months to your secret retreat, RV, or tiny home type of structure and find that it was broken into and ransacked, or even worse. Remoteness and not being on site for long periods is a perfect invitation for criminals to have the time and privacy to do as they wish to your property, regardless of how many locks you put on the gate. If you are going to leave your stuff unattended, at least place some decent cameras to see who may be visiting while you are away. If you cannot get a decent data signal that will alert you remotely, try to hide the onsite recording cameras so they will not be easily seen or tampered with. It is still a good idea to place a camera or two and some signs warning of live video monitoring as a deterrent.

If you do have electricity and a decent data connection, there are plenty of smart home technologies available, such as driveway beams, video doorbells, security lighting, and motion-activated cameras that alert you in real time and allow you to talk back or sound an alarm to scare off intruders. These may seem counter-intuitive for the place designed to be a safe haven, but security is important when you put so much time, money, and effort into preparing your little slice of heaven in the woods. At the very least, try to keep the place looking like someone is regularly there by not allowing mail or newspapers to pile up. Leave a car or two in the driveway and perhaps a big set of work boots on the porch and large dog bowls in view of the street.

If there is a road, trail, path, or sign of travel by anyone out of the ordinary, the locals will see it. When you improve the property, driveway, or road going to your new retreat, it will raise interest in what you are doing. Most likely the place you intend to buy will not have had much activity in some time, especially if it is remote. Roads and trails invite traffic by vehicle, bicycle, and even on foot. Gates and keep-out signs can raise suspicion among the locals, and possibly law enforcement, for that matter.

There can be traffic you are not aware of in your area and maybe on your property. Dog walkers, hunters, hikers, and especially kids all move about people's property all the time. Rather than wonder if it could happen, it would be better to just expect it to happen. This way of thinking will help you stay sharp about keeping things out of sight and also reduce your surprise when you see someone moving around out there, giving you a better chance to respond appropriately. You also do not want to accidentally injure someone with your buried man trap filled with punji sticks. Save those defenses for the apocalypse.

WISDOM TIP

Keep in mind that it is unsafe and most likely against the law in your area to set up anything that can intentionally harm somebody else. As long as there is rule of law, you need to reserve your man trap, tripwire, and drone machine gun fantasies for the Mad Max future we all read about on the internet. This is not to say you are not allowed to plan for such an occurrence. Some defenses are worth planning ahead of time, and there is nothing wrong with purchasing and properly storing legal materials for resourceful use in the future. Just do not put those thoughts into action quite yet. Accidents can and do happen all the time, and as soon as they do, regret usually follows. If your sharks with laser defenses actually hurt someone, your next hardened protective structure might be a prison cell.

CHAPTER 7

SURVIVAL GROUPS AND YOUR NEW RETREAT LOCATION

A survival group or team is nothing more than a number of people who realize that there is safety in numbers and wish to pool their skills and supplies in a way to support each other. In the military, you might call this a force multiplier. Survival on your own can be extremely difficult because there can be so incredibly much to do on a daily basis, and we all need to sleep sometime. If you are on your own and become injured or sick, you might not have any help to reach out to.

In the military or emergency management operations, the government has what is termed "reach back capability." This means they have the ability to ask for assistance and mutually support each other if the emergency event exceeds their local capabilities. Our nation's entire protective posture is based on the theory that all disasters or emergency events are localized, but the system has assets to respond in incredible ways up the food chain if necessary. While we as survivors need only worry about our own families, a survival group can provide this same emergency response type of function, just on a much smaller scale.

Survival groups are a great protective resource, but when it comes to getting everyone together, a number of things must be planned and communicated to the members. The group leader or leadership council needs to realize that this move will likely result in a loss of members. This is because of distance to the property, costs involved, and perhaps, some people do not like change. A survival group's primary mission is to operate under challenging conditions. If you lose people over inability to change, they may not have been right for the group in the first place. That is just the harsh reality of survival. With that being said, people need stability and to feel as if they are an important component in a larger machine. The decision to locate or relocate a group will be far more successful if the leadership presents a solid vision of why the move is a good idea, and achieving buy-in of the members will go a long way toward success.

THE BASICS

You need to understand the basics of a survival group if you are considering such a move. Every approved member of the group enters what is called the survival marriage. This simply means that if a member joins the group, you are accepting that this person, and his or her family, has the potential to spend the apocalypse with you and your children.

Choosing the best people to join your group is the number one most important task your group will ever do. Many groups overlook the baggage that comes with every new member, and that is family. We say baggage, but only for a lack of a better description. Everyone has challenges with family; it is what it is, and introducing a family to a group situation will reveal personality challenges. Of course, the challenges can be overcome, but the reality is that some people will never have good chemistry. When the survival marriage breaks up, the spurned survivalist and his or her loyal associates may take more than just half of your stuff.

A big challenge to many groups is the proximity to each other and the place they train. Most people do not want to drive very far to be in a group. If you are planning to buy a property for the group that is hours away, many will never show up, at least, not for regular group events. But rest assured, they will find their way to you if blue skies turn gray. That will be a problem. If you plan a remote retreat location for the group, take the time to survey each member to see if they will be making the journey if something bad happens. Hopefully, they will be honest with you and indicate if they will be going somewhere else. There is nothing wrong with having members who will not be relocating to the new retreat. Most disaster events will have people staying close to home, and those group members can be valuable in many other capacities, including intelligence and resource supply gathering from the home city, if needed.

When you are searching for a place to put a group, the size of the building(s), resources, and land will come into play. If you are planning to grow food to support the group or raise animals, you must consider the quality of the soils, level of ground, climate, unblocked sunlight, proximity to water, and other natural resources. If your expected attendance is more than a dozen or so individuals, you will want to have several acres devoted to food production. It is always better to plan for more than you need due to crop failures and bartering. If you are concerned about a long-term grid down or disaster environment, you should figure out how to create things of value, whether it be food, products, or services.

Some of the larger groups of several dozen upward to hundreds will form co-ops by purchasing farms or homesteads in proximity to each other, thereby owning the whole area to the extent that they have the say as to what happens in the area or region. This usually doesn't just happen. More often, the existing community forms a bond and handles things the way they all agree on. It is not impossible to find such communities that look after each other, but it does take some work to be more than just tolerated. You will need to show your value and participate as a good neighbor. Try hard, but not too hard.

Larger land requires more work and maintenance. A group should have no trouble with this. The best thing to do is list what needs to be done, what improvements you want to make, and sensible priorities. This is called establishing priorities of work. This simple process is invaluable in all things we do, especially survival work when resources are limited. When it comes to groups buying in on land together, there are some legal considerations I will address later. When you think of larger land, think of how will you protect it and any resources that are outside of the limits of your immediate living area. For example, if you own 20 acres but your water pond, spring, or livestock are on the opposite side of the property, do you have the manpower to manage the safety and security of those resources?

COMPOUNDS AND MULTIPLE STRUCTURES

For the serious-minded group with more people than can comfortably fit in a typical house, perhaps something larger would be appropriate. In my experience consulting with survival groups of various sizes, I've found that one of the bigger challenges aside from personality conflict has to do with accommodations. Privacy, space, access to toilets and shower facilities, and access to eating and food-preparation areas can all cause virtual chokepoints and personal space issues.

While a bunkhouse might work for hunters for a few days or barracks or military troops, those lodging styles require strong personal discipline, leadership, responsibility, and compromise. These are all the things that typical families struggle with, and if you put multiple families together in tight spaces, tempers usually flare. Mix this with the well-known fact that not everyone gets along, no matter how much team-building you do. Personal dynamics and chemistry have their limits. In the immortal words of Francis from the movie *Stripes*, "You touch my stuff and I kill ya, you call me Francis and I kill ya." Okay, lighten up, Francis.

A possible answer to this space problem is logically to provide more space. You can do this in a few ways: get a bigger house, provide more sleeping spaces, such as additional structures on the property, or provide everyone with their own campsite with sufficient hygiene facilities to serve the crowd during rush hours until something else can be done.

I covered house sizes earlier in the book, so let's move to additional lodging options. The large family or survival group will need enough property to give everyone space to live for the longer term if this is your plan. Since building a compound is generally a little more than most people think about, I am going to establish what this takes. Try not to get wrapped around the axle with the word "compound"; there are plenty of awesome multi-structure properties that are technically compounds. People visit them all the time for vacation, such as when staying at a bed and breakfast with a petting zoo, a wellness center with a central gathering spot and gardens, or a ranch with cabin and camping areas during a hunting trip.

HOW MUCH LAND DO YOU NEED?

So, how much land should a group have? This, of course, depends on how close everyone wants to be to each other. For the long-term survival group, space is required for food production (gardening, livestock), housing, storage of supplies and equipment, parking, and ideally, a security buffer around all the structures. We can break it down in a simple way by looking at how much space a family of four would need at a minimum and then multiply by as many families as needed.

One family needs at least a campsite-sized space for lodging. At the minimum, this should be 20 x 20 feet. Add to that a garden big enough to provide food during a growing season. This is a trickier measurement, but with good planning and experience in growing, it can be done on a quarter of an acre, which measures out to roughly 110 x 110 feet. You probably need parking space, so add another 20 x 10 feet per vehicle. If you have some small livestock such as chickens or rabbits, add space for them that's separate from the gardens because chickens can tear up a new garden very quickly. Add another 10 x 10 feet minimum for the animals, preferably more, if possible, but remember this is just for one family space. As you add families, you can combine spaces for group interdependence.

So now, let's add up the space so far:

Campsite = 400 square feet

Garden =12,100 square feet

One car parking = 200 square feet

Small livestock = 100 square feet

Total: 12,800 square feet

Total space for one family of four, as a bare minimum, is 12,800 square feet or about one third of an acre. Does this mean that 1 acre can sustain three families of four, or 12 people? It would be a big challenge requiring gardening success, and one would have to be really good with rabbits to have one in the pot each week. One large roaster rabbit feeds about five people due to its high density protein and low-fat meat.

As mentioned earlier, you can combine spaces in a compound type of environment. If you can find a property of about 5 acres, this would give you some fudge room for the garden because anyone who knows about growing their own food also knows that when things go wrong, people can get hungry. Five acres should also give you some space to spread out, possibly have a pond for your water needs, and ramp up your small livestock operation. Some things to keep in mind:

- How much space is actually usable?
- Is the land level?
- Does it have available sunlight for the entire garden?
- Are there too many trees?

The characteristics of the property will have a significant impact on group sustainability. In order to get 5 usable acres, you might need to purchase 10 or more acres.

SITE PLANNING FOR THE GROUP OR COMPOUND

The survival group can work with an empty piece of land as long as they do some planning to identify where things will go before people start showing up and claiming the best places to set up their camps. If the group fails to establish some form of site plan, there will be no order and people will get frustrated. It is recommended that careful consideration go into the site plan, because once it is established, it will be difficult to change later. Every site plan for a compound with multiple homesteads should have these common components:

- Well-defined perimeter
- Two or more gated entrances/exits
- Clear buffer space between the perimeter and all structures, for security
- Bunkhouse/lodging areas
- Toilets/hygiene areas
- Storage area/barn
- Garden/crop area
- Livestock pens/shelter
- Headquarters/radio post
- Medical bay
- Indoor group gathering location/classroom
- Outdoor gathering area/firepit
- Water feature

- Vehicle parking
- Training area/range

The key to a site plan is security, convenience, and traffic management. Place the important equipment and supplies toward the center of the camp or compound. This makes it easier to keep track of where things are and move out quickly, should the need arise. Design from the center outward then adjust the spacing of the components as needed, but don't stop there. Leave room for expansion as the group settles in. Try to leave as much room as possible for growing food.

Since this property is intended as a place where people may stay for an extended period to perform all the necessary tasks and duties of a village that may have only itself to count on in times of trouble, it is wise to understand the priorities of survival. I wouldn't advise scribbling out a site plan on a napkin and calling it a day. Review the Eight Main Areas of Survival listed in Chapter 2 as you think about your potential site plan.

Security: Security is the first and most important task that needs to be managed. It is easier to implement your security plan when there is a logical flow and arrangement to the compound. If all the residents were quartered in one area, you would lose additional eyes at the other end of the compound. By spreading people out, you increase the number of eyes and ears within the perimeter. If a security patroller were to run into trouble, the noise would be more easily heard by someone and the alarm could be spread more quickly.

Sleeping arrangements: Lodging can be accomplished in several ways. The most affordable and simple method is the tent. Most of today's tents are made for short-duration use and will begin to deteriorate with several weeks of constant use. Another option might be to set up yurts. They are more expensive but still more affordable than permanent structures or RVs, in most cases. Yurts have a lot of room, are comfortable, are usable in most climates, and are pretty easy to construct.

Of course, there is always at least one family that has a camper or RV. There is nothing wrong with that unless they run their generator and air conditioning all night while the tenters are sweating it out with the generator noise reminding them of how comfortable the RV campers are in their bunks with the TV on. While it is not really fair to the RV campers to tell them they cannot run their equipment just because people in tents do not have the same amenities, you may want to consider having them park away from the tenters out of respect. When you design your site plan, try to get a feel for how many RV campers and tenters you might have, and plan accordingly.

Toilets and showers: Any time you have a group of people in one place overnight, you will need to plan for bathrooms and

Yurt

showers. Anyone who has ever been camping knows that getting up in the middle of the night to go to the bathroom is no fun. This is made even worse when you have to put on shoes and walk two football fields away in the dark. And if it is raining or cold, it gets old really, really quick. Your site plan should provide a bathhouse close to the sleeping and gathering areas. If the eating area is the gathering area, you can combine the restroom requirements. If not, then you may need to add more restrooms. The same requirement goes for the training area if it is more than a few minutes' walk away.

There is the option of a portable restroom, but these are generally rented from a third-party company, such as those hired for construction sites or public festivals. If something happened that prevented the company from cleaning them out, you would be on your own. The other option is a good, old-fashioned outhouse. Just be sure you keep a significant distance between any toilet facilities and your water sources. Since there is plenty of information on waste disposal elsewhere, I will not get into those designs here.

Command post: The next important component to place is the command post, headquarters, or "head shed" for the group. Even Boy Scouts keep a headquarters located in the center of their large camps. This is where everything is managed, including security, radio communications, medical care, duty rosters, intelligence gathering, and all operations planning. The command post should be located toward the center of the property and well-secured. All of the important information and more valuable equipment is usually kept here.

WISDOM TIP

The HQ should be manned 24 hours a day when people are at the retreat, or at least, someone should be available on call in case of emergency. If the head shed is not manned, there should be a named alternate on the premises with a radio that can be reached at all times.

Gardening and livestock: Gardens and animals should be located close to each other because there is a lot of overlap in those operations. Ideally, these components would be located close to the water source, but take care to keep all manure away from the water source. This includes keeping rainwater runoff from places where the animals drop their manure. You must keep your water source as clean as possible and not allow fecal matter, chemicals, or oils to contaminate it. Waterborne pathogens and bacteria are not something anyone wants in their water.

When planning the food-growing areas, be aware of the available daily sunlight as it shines during the spring through fall growing season. If you live in a climate that can sustain a winter crop, keep in mind that the sun is much lower in the southern sky in the winter months. You will want plenty of sun covering the gardens for as much of the day as possible, and any trees or structures that cast shade on the garden might prevent plant growth.

Parking: Parking for vehicles should be consolidated in a designated place, preferably near the entrance, depending on the property size and layout. It is not ideal for parking to be on the far side of the camp or placed at every campsite, unless there is a safe way to allow this to happen.

Moving vehicles around campsites is a recipe for disaster. If a vehicle needs to be moved within the camp area, there should be designated lanes and walking personnel to assist the vehicle for safe movement, especially at night when people may be out in the dark or on the ground in sleeping bags, or when children are running around. Ground guides should carry bright flashlights at night, and the driver should give them decent clearance.

GATHERING AREAS

Every compound should have gathering areas for the group. Ideally, there would be an indoor and an outdoor space large enough for everyone. The indoor space is great for meetings and sharing information during inclement weather, and the outdoor space can boost morale when the weather cooperates. The outdoor gathering space would benefit from having a large fire pit and amphitheater-style seating, if possible. People will be more inclined to socialize if their seating forces them into closer proximity. Sometimes, when people bring their own chairs, they form closed circles with their usual friends and make it difficult for others to join in. By creating a fire pit at the center of the seating area and at a lower elevation, the people seated behind the first row can also see the fire and feel like part of the group.

TRAINING AREAS AND WEAPONS RANGES

A training area is also a great idea if your property has room. Most survival-minded groups like to do outdoor training, such as food foraging, tactical movements, or even firearms and archery. A wooded area is a great place to do some of these things, but to shoot anything, you need a clear lane long enough to accommodate whatever weapons you are using. There are many safety requirements for this, including making sure that no projectile leaves the intended range lanes or goes beyond the end of the target area. In other words, shoot straight and do not place your range in such a way that projectiles will continue past your range and hit a neighbor's property or roadway in the distance.

Also, be very careful about anyone wandering into the line of fire from the woods. Carefully establish fencing with ribbon and signage so that anyone moving around can clearly see the potential danger ahead. Shooters can become focused on targets and not immediately see a child walk into a firing lane. This goes for pets, as well. Place your range and outdoor training area away from other camp operations for safety.

The survival of the individual members means the survival of the group, and the group is there to protect the members. This means that as long as everyone is looking out for each other, the group will perform its core mission of protecting everyone. Along with the people in the group, equipment and supplies need to be cared for.

I will wrap up the compound design and site-planning discussion with this final note: Take care in how you lay out the site

plan, and use common sense. Keep vehicles in safe areas, keep waste away from food and water sources, store the important items near the center of the perimeter, and place people in such a way that they enhance the security plan, not require a bigger security plan. Arrange components in such a way that less labor is required to performing daily tasks, such carrying water.

GROUP PURCHASES OF PROPERTY

There are several ways to purchase a property, and while I cannot explain them all, I can give you some things to think about before you get some friends to go all in on the property of your dreams. Any time you introduce another person and his or her money to your idea, you risk disharmony. People have a way of agreeing on how great things can be when the idea is just that, an idea. But once the chips are down and hard-earned money is on the table, it usually has some strings attached. The worse news is that those strings may not be easily cut. If you have ever pooled your money to buy something with a friend and then found out that the thing you pitched in to buy was either not available or broken when you wanted to use it, you know what I am talking about.

If you really think that involving other people in this purchase is a good idea, you will need to treat it as a business deal. This could mean considering some different types of legal agreements, such as a land trust or possibly establishing an LLC. This requires involving a real estate attorney and setting up the proper financials with an experienced accountant. This is by no means a recommendation for any particular method or arrangement, and I am not an attorney with experience in these areas, but a land purchase is a long-term, high-dollar purchase with serious ramifications if things go wrong, an injury on the property happens, or circumstances, such as the death of a partner or owner, force a change of ownership.

Given the legal problems that can go unseen for some time, it is strongly recommended that you secure a real estate attorney who is familiar with the specific area you are looking to purchase in. There are various other reasons to consult with counsel, such as finding ways to title the property without your name being made public, as well as asset management and protection.

If you are already an individual owner of the property, you may have people who wish to buy in or invest in the land. For many of the same reasons I already touched on, I do not recommend allowing this as it could come back to haunt you if the relationship were to turn sour.

Depending on how large your group is, you may look for some sort of agreement that clarifies property ownership but allows others to volunteer or donate in some fashion to the group. Many groups charge dues to help with expenses; if this is something your group is considering, be sure to already have strong, effective leadership in place for the group. Make it clear that the dues are to be used in accordance with the policies and procedures established by the group and that in no way does the payment of dues constitute any real property ownership unless otherwise legally documented. Gear or equipment would normally be owned by the lender and goes with the lender if he or she leaves the group, unless otherwise arranged.

HE DIED AND LEFT IT TO WHO?!

There are cases where people who have bought in and become a legal owner of the property pass away, leaving ownership to family or an estate. This presents an unusual predicament for the serious survival group. What happens when the potentially unknown beneficiary wishes to use the land with his or her friends, yet they have nothing to do with the survival group? What does a group who took so much care in vetting members do now that strangers want to ride dirt bikes and party on their group land? What if the inheritors want to sell their newly found stake but the group cannot afford to buy it back?

A divorce can also be complicated when assets are divided and the property is one of those assets. Especially when the divorcees hate each other but still want to be in the group and use the property. These are scenarios the serious survival group may want to consider and retain counsel on before pooling their personal money to buy a property.

When I am asked about others putting money into someone else's property, I recommend that the property owner make the financial investment into the property improvements and allow the others to volunteer their time and labor with the understanding that regardless of what happens, at the end of the day, the actual documented owner is the only owner. This comes off as a form of sweat equity and may earn the volunteer a symbolic place in the group, but does not guarantee any formal ownership of the property or permanent structures associated with it. Again, anyone can sue and there is always a lawyer out there somewhere who may accept the challenge, so it is wise to get some good legal advice before allowing anyone to assist or invest in real property improvements.

LEGAL CONSIDERATIONS

This country is enmeshed in a patchwork of laws and customs, and while we usually move through our day not seeing the differences in ordinances from one town to another, that is usually because we just don't get caught doing something that was always okay somewhere else. A simple example would be knife or gun laws. The gun laws are a very popular area of disagreement among people nationwide, but we rarely hear of someone getting in trouble over a pocket knife. That is, until you get caught carrying something you always thought was okay in your hometown when visiting or house hunting, for example, in another town or state. There is a long list of differences in types of pocket knives, how they open, how long the blade can be, etc. While you did not intend to break the law, you could be considered a criminal and have no idea.

The same goes for things like rain barrels. One city may give you a water bill discount and a free rain barrel to help conserve water, while the town next door will penalize you with a fine for using a rain barrel, calling it water theft if you harvest rain. These situations seem to defy logic and certainly make no sense, but if you are looking to settle down somewhere and such matters are important to you, it would be appropriate to ask some questions to the people who enforce such laws.

Survival preparation includes many skills and tasks that fall outside of daily modern society, such as raising livestock, growing a garden, and living without a grid connection. Some or all of these are not accepted in many places; they may be outright illegal in other communities. There are many stories of self-reliant folk being fined, evicted, and even imprisoned just for trying to live life on their own terms. If you are looking to relocate to a new area it is very important to gain an understanding of the rules in that area.

When considering a new community or state, look into legal or HOA restrictions for hobbies or operations related to self-reliance in the following areas:

- Gardens
- Animals
- Electrical generation, solar panels, wind turbines, etc.
- Disconnecting from grid
- Rain harvesting
- Aquaponics systems
- Irrigation restrictions
- Hunting
- Fishing
- Trapping
- Storage structures
- Buried structures

- Ham radio antennas
- Additional vehicles, unregistered off-road vehicles
- Trucks, boats, etc.
- Gun laws
- Knife laws
- Camp fires, fire pits, etc.
- Mineral rights, water, etc.
- Tree cutting, land clearing
- Construction
- Personal drone/UAS (Unmanned Aircraft Systems) flying
- Forming tactical style groups, allowing rank structure
- Tactical training, individual or groups
- Property ownership, individual or groups

When you are looking for that place to settle down and be allowed to do all the things you want to do, the last thing you want is to end up running afoul of the law. You already know for the most part what kind of things you want to do at your new property; all you need to do is some due diligence to make sure you don't end up frustrated or in a legal fight because you were not aware of some restriction. Use the above list as a primer to become informed.

LIABILITY, THE SPECTER OF FINANCIAL DOOM

This leads us to the next concern as a property owner: liability. Everyone hates lawyers until someone gets hurt or something breaks. Well, lawyers are still hated then, too, but they are better suited to bring the legal system to bear than the rest of us. Usually. We all would like to operate safely and in a manner that prevents injury and property damage, but in the dangerous world of survival, bad things can happen. You need to make every effort to provide a safe environment free of neglect as a property owner or skill trainer. Physical safety is only part of the story. You may want to think about other forms of protection as a backup plan just in case something bad does happen.

Most of us have some form of insurance, such as health, car, and homeowners policies, but if you are purchasing a property or home for the purpose of inviting others over to train for survival or build a mini-farm on an empty lot, what happens if someone gets injured? Survival includes a lot of knives, fire, tools, physical exertion, vehicles, firearms, and other potentially hazardous acts. If someone gets injured, the property owner could be at risk of lawsuit for damages, regardless if everyone involved is friends, possibly even family. It would not hurt to make every effort to protect yourself and your family as much as possible by having appropriate liability insurance if you can get it.

Since the world has not ended yet, you as the new property owner can be held responsible for what happens on your property. When providing, allowing, or facilitating training on your property, make every effort to be responsible by only providing appropriate training by people who hold approved training requirements and possibly by requiring signed waivers to enter the property and or participate in such activities. If someone wants to teach a skill that could be dangerous, ask yourself, "Is this person really qualified to do this, and are all appropriate safety measures being taken?" These are some examples a qualified attorney may recommend as a comprehensive package to keep everyone protected.

CHAPTER 8

WHITTLING DOWN THE SHORT LIST OF PROPERTIES

There is a lot of information to consider for the relocation process and it may not be practical to apply everything I have offered to your search. You will probably look at so many properties that they'll all begin to blend together. To avoid this, I recommend you take a notepad and scribble some notes about any property you like so you can compare later. It helps to have a solid idea of what you are looking for, but it is okay to change your expectations midstream if you are not having any luck. You might make your real estate agent a little nuts, but it is your money, and as long as you respect the agent's time, you should be okay. Do not feel pressured to make an offer on something just because you looked at 15 properties. Our agent stuck with me for almost 70 properties until I found the right one. This can happen when you are looking at an unfamiliar market in rapidly changing conditions. I sent his family gifts as a peace offering.

When you find a few places that can be seriously considered for purchase but cannot make a decision, sit down with your decision team, take out your notes and any photos you took, and do the pros and cons thing. If that works, great, but if you are still undecided, do not fear. You have options. Naturally, there is some math involved, which is appropriate because you are trying to keep the emotional quotient low here. Do not worry, it will be very simple math.

Here is a simple method you can use to determine what is important and how your short list of properties compare. It is called a comparison table. You can scribble it out on a napkin if you want, but I would recommend at least using a notepad. Either way, it does not get much easier than this. You use this simple decision tool to compare all kinds of choices.

THE COMPARISON TABLE

Wants and Needs	Property #1	Pts	Property #2	Pts	Property #3	Pts
Work commute?	20 minutes	5	45 minutes	1	30 minutes	4
Quality of schools?	6 out of 10	6	5 out of 10	5	8 out of 10	8
Size of house?	1,200 SF	2	1,800 SF	4	2,700 SF	10
Size of property?	½ acre	2	1 acre	8	1 ¼ acres	9
Age of house?	12 years	4	15 years	3	4 years	9
Price?	$185K	10	$205K	10	$280K	4
7-year resale value?	Median	5	Lower	4	Higher	8
Point total		34		35		52

The idea of a comparison table is simple.

- On the left column of the table, write the things you want or need to find in a property. These would be the things that are most important to you.
- On the top row of the table, list the houses or properties you are seriously considering and would actually purchase. Just the exercise of adding a property to the list could be enough for you to dismiss it for some unconscious reason. See, it's working already! Besides, you knew that one-bedroom cabin wasn't realistic anyway; your wife probably made that pretty clear.
- In the body of the table, answer the questions from the left side. Next to each answer, assign a number of points from 1 to 10, 1 being the lowest match and 10 being the closet match to what you are looking for.
- Add up the numbers in each column. The highest score is the property that offers you the closest match to what you described as important to you.

This table presents the best compromise of the three selected properties. While one or two of your desired characteristics may score higher or lower in the selected property, this is an overall score to help you get a clear picture of which choice has the most to offer.

In the sample table, I created a list of things you might be looking for while shopping. For example, you might want a newer home approximately 2,700 square feet, 10 minutes away from work, on at least an acre of land in a good school district. Your preferred budget might be $250K, but for the right house, you are comfortable going up to $295K as a firm high limit. You understand that as a general rule, every one thousand dollars adds roughly six dollars to your monthly mortgage. So for the right house at the higher end of your price range, your payment would increase by roughly $270 per month. But if this means you are not spending $45K or more on a renovation at a higher lending rate, you'd be okay with that. Of course, in this scenario, this more expensive home really needs to score much higher in the resale category to be worth it to you in case you want to sell in the future.

WISDOM TIP

I have seen too many people who stretched out their financial necks and have been stuck in an aging home for a long time, unable to sell for what they owe. To make matters worse, their mortgage payment is too high and the resale value is too low, since they never had enough money to upgrade or maintain their home. Their 1996 home still looks just like it did in 1996, only a lot older and way out of style.

In this comparison scenario, I find that the initial desires turned out to be unrealistic in that particular market location. To find the home I wanted with a larger lot and better schools, I needed to look farther away from the commute target to a newer developing area or change the expectations and decide if an older, smaller home was going to work for us. Newer homes in the farther-out, growing community would cost a little more but also offer better resale, and since the new area was growing so fast, I find that commuting to the original area is less important. These are all things worth considering.

To make a comparison table work properly, you need to sit down and make a list of important criteria that you want in a home or property. The list should be prioritized with important requirements first and desirable characteristics after that. The list can be as long as you like but the more items you add, the more you might dilute the important requirement scores if you start to give high scores to things like pretty flower beds and a south-facing front door. Try to stick to things that really are important, such as less than 10 minutes to the grocery store, reasonable commute to work, or overall condition of the structure.

If you have a spell of inspiration and can make the list in one quick sitting, that is fine, but this might be something you want to start on a notepad and add to over time. You can revise and update the list even as you are actively looking at houses and properties, because by that time, you will have a better idea of what you want, what you can afford, and what the community has to offer.

Here are some starter ideas for your list; feel free to add or remove anything you want. It may help to take the list with you when scouting properties either online or in person, just to keep you focused on the job at hand.

- Proximity to family
- Proximity to necessities (shopping, medical, fire, police)
- Quality of healthcare
- Urban density
- Commute times
- Rush-hour congestion
- School quality rating
- School commute time
- Property size
- Structure size
- Floor plan/layout
- Resources on site (water, trees, hunting)
- Space to add a garden
- Available sunlight for garden
- Property border/fencing
- Proximity to faith-based resources
- Proximity to highways
- Proximity to airport

- Proximity to microbrewery (just making sure you are paying attention)
- Age and condition of home
- Potential for fortification or survival improvements
- Potential resale value
- Alternative employment opportunities nearby
- General economic conditions of the area
- Crime rates in the area
- Agreeable demographics

When you use the table and start to see the scores, take a moment and give them the sniff test. Do the results make sense? If not, maybe you didn't give the answers realistic points in the columns. Or maybe you already knew which house you wanted and gave high scores to the house you subconsciously wanted. It might be a good idea to have your partner run the same table just to see how he or she scores. You may get some interesting results, and if their scores are significantly different, you have some things to work out because this means you are not completely in agreement on what is important for this purchase. While this could be a problem, it does not have to be. As long as you agree on the important needs, and those are the everyday life needs, you can compromise on the other stuff. Just try to be as realistic and unbiased as possible when scoring. This is business right now, so try to keep the emotions at bay.

To assist you in identifying what you are looking for so you can start looking without wasting time, I have created a table of questions on the next page. You can work together or separately to answer the questions. The goal is to see how close you and your partner are to wanting the same things and where you differ. It is better to identify your differences now, while you have time to reevaluate.

COMPARISON TABLE BASIC INFORMATION WORKSHEET

Where do you want to live? State/Community	
What climate do you want? Warm, cold, mixed season	
What terrain do you want? Coast, mountain, desert, Midwest, lowland, Appalachian, plains	
What type of community? Urban, suburban, rural	
How much land? Lot size	
What size house do you want, in square feet?	
What type of house? Ranch, multistory	
How many bedrooms?	
What age house?	
What is your budget limit?	

If you are working to get your family on board with your idea of relocating, you will have better success if they feel as if they have a say in the process. When people feel as if their opinions are valued, they will be more comfortable with the process and more supportive. If you find stiff resistance to the moving process, it could be out of fear of trying something different or it could be that they just want something different than you. Give them a chance to join in the process, ask what they think, and give them a reason to support your idea. Young kids are one thing but your spouse is something else altogether. If you want to keep your relationship intact, work as a team and not as a dictatorship.

Use the information gleaned from the table to set the basis for your search. Something will likely change but that is the evolution of the process. At least you will all be in general agreement of where to start.

Keep this information close as you shop and refer back to it to keep you focused. If you find that you are having trouble getting close to what you want, you may have to adapt your wants or look somewhere else. Once you have a couple of purchase options in mind, then go ahead and crank up the comparison table.

WRAPPING IT ALL UP

The process of relocating, whether it is for a permanent move or to prepare a survival retreat, is not something to be taken lightly. You will have an easier time of it if you do some prep work up front and lay the groundwork. Very few people make the move by themselves; others will be affected and should be included. You family is most likely your core survival group and this fact will not change no matter the situation. Get their input, value it, and include them as much as possible, because survival is all about working with what you have, and those resources include the people who will be alongside of you the entire way.

The time to get started is now. Where do you dream of going?

PHOTO CREDITS

Page 8 © DR Travel Photo and Video

Page 12 © Globe Guide Media Inc.

Page 15 © Theeraphong

Page 18 © WDG Photo

Page 33 © Greg and Jan Ritchie

Page 35 © Roman Babakin

Page 36 © Anton Backsholm

Page 44 © vincent noel

Page 56 © Radovan1

Page 59 © Maxim Petrichuk

Page 75 © PGMart

Page 79 © Rudra Narayan Mitra

Page 82 © scubaluna

Page 85 © Phillip Minnis

Page 91 © Litwin Photography

Page 101 © ABC Photo

Page 105 © Paul Brennan

Page 115 © UTBP

Page 119 © GoodMood Photo

Page 122 © Nutchanart Wong-onsri

Page 123 © J.D.S

Page 126 © KPG_Payless

Page 128 © Kelly MacDonald

Page 132 © Photographicss

Page 144 © Aumphotography

Page 148 © Daengpanya Atakorn

Page 153 © Steven Frame

ABOUT THE AUTHOR

© Courtney Hogwood

As a Lead Scout with the 11th Armored Cavalry, U.S. Army, Charley Hogwood spent years deployed in Europe honing his skills in reconnaissance, surveillance, and humanitarian missions. As an active member of the U.S. Army, he was charged with border security operations, including planning and participating in patrolling and security operations, rapid reaction deployment, and security of several international incidents.

After serving in the U.S. Army, he returned to Florida and began working in construction, focusing on project management, utility infrastructure, and residential upgrades. As a licensed general contractor and home inspector, he's spent the last 30 years honing his skills in both residential and commercial real estate, including work in renovations, remodeling, and building inspections. In addition, he is a certified commercial drone pilot, holding an FAA Part 107 License. His use of the latest in drone technology has given him the ability to provide in-depth analyses of homes and neighborhoods for property buyers as they embark on the home-buying process.

In addition to his work in construction, Charley has spent the last 10 years working as a preparedness consultant. Whether it's an individual looking to start their prepping adventure or a group looking to build an intentional community, Charley has helped them plan, search, and build their dream survival destinations.

Charley is the author of *The Survival Group Handbook: How To Plan, Organize and Lead People for Short and Long Term Survival*, the foremost guide to planning, organizing, and building a survival group for any situation. His book has been utilized by small and large groups alike, and has also been used as a team-building resource for both corporations and civilian organizations.

Charley has completed hundreds of hours of emergency preparedness training at the local, state, and federal levels. He holds a certificate in emergency management, has over 55 FEMA/DHS certificates, and has completed coursework in disaster readiness, business contingency and continuity planning, emergency operations policies and procedures, mass prophylaxis planning, nuclear WMD responder operations, rapid disaster impact assessment, volunteer management, and more. As a CERT team leader and instructor, he has undergone additional training in disaster preparedness, fire suppression, medical triage, search and rescue, disaster psychology, and terrorism threats.